PERFORMING SHAKESPEARE

Kenneth Branagh as Hamlet in the RSC's production of Hamlet, *1992.*
(Photo: Robbie Jack)

PERFORMING SHAKESPEARE

John Hester

THE CROWOOD PRESS

First published in 2008 by
The Crowood Press
Ramsbury, Marlborough
Wiltshire SN8 2HR

www.crowood.com

All photographs are by the author, with the exception of pages 2, 7, 9, 21, 33, 42, 61, 75, 102, 123 and 136 © Robbie Jack.

Front cover: Frances Barber (as Cleopatra) and Nicholas Jones (as Antony) in *Antony and Cleopatra* at the Globe Theatre in London. © Robbie Jack.

Back cover: Andrea Harris (as Titania) and Joe Dixon (as Bottom) in the RSC's production of *A Midsummer Night's Dream* at the Courtyard Theatre, Stratford-Upon-Avon. © Robbie Jack.

British Library Cataloguing-in-Publication Data
A catalogue record for this book is available from the British Library.

ISBN 978 1 84797 073 2

Dedication
To my father Allan Hester – much loved '*best of men*'.

The play *Down and Out with Bill Shakespeare* on pages 137–150 remains the copyright of the author, who should be duly acknowledged in the programme notes of any performance.

Typeset by Carolyn Griffiths, Cambridge
Printed and bound in Singapore by Craft Print International

CONTENTS

ACKNOWLEDGEMENTS

A special thank you to the Art Educational Schools London, for the loan of one of their studios as a venue for many of the photographs in this book, and also to their headmaster Oliver Price. As both a vocational school and college they continue to display extraordinary levels of excellence and professionalism. Thanks also to Sutton Theatres where my Spats Theatre School is located.

Thanks also to the Performing Shakespeare Ensemble, who appear in the photographs: ex-students of Newlands School – Briony Price, Janina Smith and Eleanor Young; and from Spats Theatre School – Jade Elise Campkin, Alex Donnachie, Stephanie Hawthorne and Keiran Laurie.

INTRODUCTION

Judi Dench as Mistress Quickly in the RSC's Merry Wives –
the Musical, *2007. (Photo: Robbie Jack)*

INTRODUCTION

The aim of this book is to introduce you to the exciting and fascinating world of performing the work of the greatest playwright that ever lived – and is ever likely to. William Shakespeare is known throughout the world as the creator of the very finest dramatic literature and poetry. To watch a well-crafted production of a Shakespeare play is one of the most fulfilling artistic experiences to be had, but to be part of one and to participate in the long-established tradition of interpreting his work for yet another generation is both a privilege and a joy.

It will be obvious to you from the start that performing Shakespeare is not, generally, an activity that you can undertake on your own. However, it may well be that you are reading this book with the intention of developing a repertoire of Shakespearean audition pieces and, if this is the case, you should find this book an ideal tool. However, although much of the text and many of the exercises are designed to be worked upon alone, you will find other parts of the book will require you to work with at least one other person in order to gain full benefit from the work.

If you are a director or workshop leader you will find the book an excellent basis for developing a programme of work, and you will find that even the individual exercises can be undertaken by members of a group observing and commenting on each others progress.

If you are an actor who is keen to perform Shakespeare, the book will serve as a safe and secure introduction for you, enabling you to build your skill and knowledge in the comfort of your own home. However, do not delay too long in putting what you learn into practice, and seek out fellow enthusiasts with whom to work as soon as you feel confident enough to do so.

The book has many exercises spaced throughout the text. Ideally, you should attempt these as you go along. However, if you do not feel comfortable with this immediately, just read them along with the other parts of the text as they contain information and suggestions that you will need even if you are not approaching the work practically for the time being. Remember though that, although there is much to be gained from simply reading the book, it is really designed as a practical tool and, therefore, you should attempt as many of the exercises as you can. Ideally, you should incorporate them into an ongoing programme of work that will gradually build and extend your skills.

Whoever you are, and whatever your reasons for using this book – whether you are an amateur, professional, student or complete beginner – whether you wish to go to drama school, get a job with a classical theatre company or form your own fringe ensemble – the most important thing to remember is to approach the book with a sense of fun and adventure. The book is designed to appeal and be useful to a large range of people with a diverse set of needs, but its most important criteria is that of enjoyment. Shakespeare has provided us with the most amazing leisure pursuit: one that can certainly be enjoyed as a spectator but one that can offer immense pleasure and challenges to the performer too.

So clear your mind, clear a space and get ready to work. The road ahead is probably an easier one than you presently imagine, but it is challenging nonetheless. Start your journey with excited anticipation and prepare to be amazed.

1 INTRODUCING THE MAN HIMSELF

Zoë Wanamaker, James Alper, Thomas Goodridge, Nicky Wardley and Simon Russell Beale in Much Ado About Nothing *at the National Theatre, 2007. (Photo: Robbie Jack)*

Before You Begin

No acting student can conduct their work in a vacuum and, prior to beginning your studies, it will be helpful, and indeed necessary, for you to possess just a little information about the life and work of the focus of your endeavours. It may well be that you already possess such information but, if you do not, it will be as well for you to spend a very small amount of time acquainting yourself with some basic facts.

This first chapter contains the very minimum you should know in order to begin an informed study of performing Shakespeare's magnificent works, and it will provide a very simple basis for you to begin with. However, do not be afraid of further enquiry elsewhere, for Shakespeare is a fascinating subject in himself and there is much interesting information about him for you to discover and digest. Information is power and this applies as much to the actor as to anyone else.

There are three main areas of attention for you here. The first is a short biographical type history of the man, then (and probably most importantly) some detail concerning theatre of the time generally (and Shakespearean Theatre specifically) and finally, two different lists of his plays – one with dates.

Shakespeare's Life and Work

Although more is known about William Shakespeare's life than any of his fellow playwrights of the time (with the exception of Ben Jonson), the amount of actual recorded and reasonably verifiable facts detailing his existence on this earth are very limited indeed. There are additional myths and legends often appended to these facts, such as that of a Stratford boy poaching deer and rabbits and subsequently fleeing to London, but these are merely traditions that may perhaps be true, or contain truth, but have absolutely no evidence to support them.

This relative lack of information about a man widely held to be the world's greatest playwright is extraordinary, particularly considering the overwhelming importance of the man historically and culturally and the astonishing influence he has had upon our understanding of human life.

The Facts

William's mother was Mary Arden, the daughter of a wealthy landowner. In around 1557 she married his father, John Shakespeare, who was a glove maker and trader. John was also something of an important figure in local politics, variously holding the positions of Constable of the Borough, Town Chamberlain, Alderman and High Bailiff – an equivalent of a modern day Mayor – in his home town of Stratford. However, it is interesting to note that, for some unknown reason, he disappears from the local political scene later on.

It is often stated that William was born on 23 April 1564 but this is not a proven fact. Although he may well have entered the world upon that day, as there is a parish record of his baptism for the 26 April that year, it is also possible that tradition has assigned that day as his birthday for the romanticized reason that he died upon that day fifty-two years later. Certainly there is no recorded verification of his actual birth at all.

It is generally assumed that William attended the Stratford grammar school although, again, there is no surviving record

The Swan Theatre in Stratford-upon-Avon.

of this stating his actual name. Here he would have received an education based firmly upon Latin and literature, but excluding maths and science.

In 1582 William married Anne Hathaway who was eight years his senior: at least, a marriage licence was issued to them in that year. They had a child the following year and twins in 1585.

It is frustrating that nothing is really known of how Shakespeare moved from Stratford to London and became an actor, for this would be information of far greater interest to students of his work than dates of birth, death and marriage. One theory is that he made the journey, originally, to become a teacher but this, again, is really only founded upon tradition and myth rather than hard fact. The first documented reference to him as a playwright was in 1592 and there are reasonable grounds to believe that he had acted before this and served at least a few years of theatrical apprenticeship.

There are also references to him continuing to act after this date, establishing that he actively operated as both actor and playwright. Although some educated men looked down upon actors of the time, it was not generally considered a disreputable occupation and, indeed, when the Shakespeare family were awarded a coat of arms in 1596 this was probably not unconnected to William's continuing success.

William worked for a theatre company called The Lord Chamberlain's Men (later to be called The King's Men under James the First), and it is believed that his acting was mainly focused upon supporting roles, such as the Ghost in *Hamlet*. The company was run by James Burbage – probably the first of the great 'Actor Managers' – aided by his sons Richard (who was the lead actor, creating many of the great Shakespearean roles) and Cuthbert (who also became his brother's manager). As playwright, Shakespeare obviously commanded influence and was probably actively involved in management as he became part owner of the Globe Theatre (built by Burbage and his sons in 1599 and where most of Shakespeare's plays were produced), with a ten per cent interest in the business – thus being the only Elizabethan actor known to have taken a share in the profits of a playhouse.

The Globe Theatre was destroyed by fire in 1612, rebuilt the following year, and then remained in use until it was demolished in 1644. It remains, historically, the most famous and important single theatre of all time, and has since been recreated in London for a modern audience still hungry for Shakespearean drama and the Elizabethan theatrical experience.

During his career Shakespeare wrote many plays (the exact number being somewhat disputed but canonically believed to be thirty seven), basically divided between comedies, tragedies and histories (all with various sources), and much poetry including the wonderful sonnets. His success brought parallel

---

Handy Hint 1

Know Your Stuff

It will not be possible for you to make a study of Shakespearean performance without a reasonably effective working knowledge of the plays. You do not have to be an expert or any kind of scholar, but you do need to know what goes on and what the basic themes are. If this is not the case, or if perhaps you could do with a little revision, List A at the end of this chapter will help you to see at a glance the treasures on offer in their three basic categories.

It will be immensely helpful to your performance work if, in parallel to it, you undertake a little gentle study of the plays. Do not let this become daunting – take it slowly and use the opportunity, when you encounter a play in one of the exercises, to focus on becoming familiar with its story.

If you become a little tired of actually reading the plays, you can always resort to film versions of which there are many great examples available. Your very best course of action, of course, is to get to see as many live theatre performances as you can. However, don't forget that, as a performer rather than just an audience member, there is no substitute for reading and, in time, you should make it your aim to devour them all.

---

financial rewards and it is generally thought that he made a considerable amount of money from his endeavours. He retired back to Stratford in 1613 and died three years later: the date of his death being attested by inscription upon a monument near to his burial place within the chancel of the church at Stratford.

In 1623 and seven years after William's death, John Heminges and Henry Condell (two important actors from the company) collected his plays together into a complete volume called the 'First Folio' which has become a major source (although not the only one) for editors ever since.

SHAKESPEARE'S THEATRE

Going to the theatre in Shakespeare's time, especially to the Globe itself, must have been an exciting an exhilarating experience. Theatre-going today is something of a refined, polite and calm affair with the ambiance of the theatre focused upon quiet concentration and measured appreciation of the play. An original Shakespearean theatrical outing must have been a very different kind of encounter with drama, and it requires a leap of imagination to appreciate its differences.

Elizabethan theatres were unroofed play-houses with a large open space for spectators, walled on three sides with galleries. The focal point was, of course, the stage, which was roofed over, with a gallery for musicians and a tower for machinery. The galleries were for those who could afford their relative shelter and the comfort of benches or stools to sit upon. Down on the main floor stood the 'groundlings', those of lesser means who would stand throughout the performance, open to the elements. It must surely have been they, enthusiastically expectant of rousing entertainment, which would have lent the Globe its unique atmosphere of theatrical anticipation.

It must be remembered that these people were not bound by the same conventions of polite appreciation and deference as twenty-first century theatre-goers. They would have most certainly been a voluble lot and their

A playhouse of today.

focus and concentration upon the play would have had to be earned by the performers and, indeed, by the playwright.

It was essential that the plays were accessible and relevant to their audience. They had to be easy to understand, immediate in the communication of their plots and themes and contain plenty of popular elements – such as excitement, comedy, tragedy, love and lust. Shakespeare was very much a commercial writer: his endeavours were not principally academic exercises but, rather, bound by the requirements of popular entertainment.

The actors too had a very important part to play in capturing and maintaining the

13

audience's attention and good will. There was no time to slowly build a rapport with them: performers had to go out upon the stage and grab their attention quickly and firmly and then keep it throughout a long play. These patrons were demanding, required entertaining and would not give their support to the performance without it being earned. If they were not happy with the fare provided they would become restless, defocused and loud – having no fears whatsoever about vocally expressing their disapproval. One can imagine the scene being something like a stand-up routine in a comedy club of today.

However, having the audience attentive and keeping their participatory involvement sympathetic to the performance was not the only reason for ensuring their appreciation of the afternoon's entertainment. The 'groundlings' did not buy tickets prior to the performance, as would happen today; neither did they pay turnstile-like as they came in. Instead, a person known as 'the Gatherer' would circulate among them as the play progressed, collecting their entrance fees, rather like someone collecting deckchair money on a beach. This was potentially disruptive in itself, but it also meant that patrons might move around somewhat as an avoidance tactic. If they were not convinced of the quality of the drama on offer they could leave before paying and so getting their attention and thus securing a fee was of very practical importance as well as artistic.

All of these various elements of place and atmosphere would have almost certainly produced a very different style of acting from that a modern audience may be used to, with less emphasis upon subtlety and detail and more upon broad, bold characterization and clearly defined situations and reactions. Laurence

Olivier made this very clear in his film of *Henry V*, in which the first act is played as a playhouse performance in the Globe, with plenty of simple, basic and naïve-like quality of acting, with the following acts morphing into a proper filmic interpretation with an appropriate change to subtlety of style more pertinent to the medium.

The construction of the play *Henry V* is a very good example of how important getting the audience's attention, and continuing to fire their excitement, actually was. The play begins with a lone actor, as Chorus, entering the stage and directly addressing the audience. He apologizes for having to tell such a magnificent tale upon so unworthy a stage, and then proceeds to feed his listener's imaginations with advocacy of the wondrous spectacle they are about to witness. It is not difficult to imagine the poor actor playing this part being firmly instructed to make sure he was dynamic, interesting and fully connected to his audience from the start, so as to 'pull them in' and convince them of the advisability of remaining in place for the rest of the play – a very pressured job indeed! Not content with this, Shakespeare has the Chorus repeating the exercise at the beginning of each of the five acts, in an attempt to ensure the audience's continued enrapture.

Visually, it is often assumed that a contemporary Shakespearean production would have been very basic and lacking in spectacle, but this is not an altogether fair assumption. Certainly there would not have been the complexity of scenery and technical wizardry that might be on display in a premier theatre today, but there is evidence of some scenery and effects including fire and smoke. It is also known that the stage would contain trap-

Something that was very different from modern theatre on the Elizabethan stage was a lack of women. There were no female actors in Shakespeare's time and the female parts would have been played by boys. In light of this, it is particularly amazing that Shakespeare chose to write so many very strong female roles and, in many instances in his work, can be seen to be demonstrating a feminist point of view that

O for a muse of fire!

doors, which were no doubt used for appropriate effects and entrances.

There was, however, no real attempt at historical accuracy made in the costuming of the productions. Actors would dress modern to their time rather than use period costume, although they might use a single item to represent the time of the play – such as a toga thrown over an otherwise inappropriate costume to represent Ancient Rome. This is rather reminiscent of the way some Shakespearean productions are staged today and certainly gives food for thought to those who criticize the use of 'modern dress' in modern interpretations of Shakespeare's works.

Handy Hint 2

Understand Shakespeare's Journey

All good artists take a professional as well as personal journey through their working lives: their early work usually differs greatly from their latter, not just in terms of quality, but also in regard to their approach and attitude to their subjects. Shakespeare is no exception to this and his progression as a writer is evident along the linear timeline of the plays.

Use List B at the end of this chapter to see just when each play was written (approximately) and how Shakespeare progressed forwards in terms of what he was writing about and how it was executed. As you become more familiar with the content of the works, so the progression will become clearer. For instance, you will note how unsophisticated, basic, raw and fundamentally sensationalist the early-ish play Titus Andronicus is compared with the later offerings – particularly *The Tempest*. It is also interesting to see how his output increased and when his most prolific period was. Use the list to formulate a slightly more academic view of Shakespeare's muse, as this will help you to begin to formulate your own opinions and theories about the works and the inspiration behind them.

Some of Shakespeare's boys made uncannily realistic women.

would not disgrace many a twentieth and twenty-first century writer.

EXERCISE – STARTING WORK

It is already time for you to commence the practical work essential to your study. The first of many exercises in this book is designed to introduce you to the power of Shakespeare's writing, and also to give you a feel for how the performer can harness and utilize that power when addressing an audience directly and thus capture and develop that audience's attention – just as the actor playing Chorus had to in those early performances of *Henry V*.

To this end you will become a different Chorus, that belonging to *Romeo and Juliet*, but one that still has the onerous task of beginning the play and speaking first. The language and verse construction is reasonably straightforward and contained within a simple sonnet but, if you are a novice, you may wish to postpone the exercise until you have worked through the chapters on voice and verse-speaking. However, start with this if you can, as it is an ideal way of launching yourself into your labours.

The Dynamic Shakespearean
Begin the task by carefully and slowly reading quietly to yourself this speech from the Prologue to *Romeo and Juliet*:

> Two households, both alike in dignity
> In fair Verona, where we lay our scene,
> From ancient grudge break to new mutiny,
> Where civil blood makes civil hands unclean.
> From forth the fatal loins of these two foes
> A pair of star-crossed lovers take their life;
> Whose misadventures piteous overthrows
> Doth with their death bury their parents'
>   strife.
> The fearful passage of their death-marked
>   love
> And the continuance of their parents rage,
> Which but their children's end, naught could
>   remove,
> Is now the two hours' traffic of our stage;
> The which if you with patient ears attend,
> What here shall miss, our toil shall strive to
>   mend.

Now read it again, but this time aloud, and using a natural level of volume for the room you are in. Do not rush and listen to the sound

Romeo and Juliet – *a more relaxed prologue.*

of the words as you speak them. Enjoy listening to yourself, however faltering your speech may be – you are already performing Shakespeare.

Spend some time assessing for yourself what the words mean (find a copy of the play with notes if you need to) and, more importantly, what they are trying to achieve. Think about how the Chorus is trying to fascinate and excite his or her audience about the story to come and to draw them into the action that is about to commence upon the stage.

With this in mind, speak the speech again, this time to an imaginary audience. Do not worry about the beauty of the words or the elegance of the verse – just think about trying to be interesting, convincing and dynamic and really try to 'sell' the story you are referring to.

Do not be vague in your imaginings – know the size and boundaries of your stage, the size of your audience and where they are. Try to look at, and include, all of them as you speak.

Finally, repeat this just once more but, in order to replicate the less than automatically attentive atmosphere of an original production, put some reasonably energetic music on – not too loud, but just loud enough that you have to raise your voice and personality above the distraction.

The last part of this exercise is most important, if a little bizarre. It should place firmly in your mind at this early stage that the job of performing Shakespeare is not just one of artistic and poetic interpretation, but also of practicality and accurate execution.

Handy Hint 3

Other Practitioners

Shakespeare was not by any means the only important playwright of his time. There were several others writing shortly before, during and after his own literary career. They include Thomas Kyd, Christopher Marlowe, Ben Jonson and (some time later) John Webster – who, as T.S. Eliot much later wrote, 'was much possessed by death and saw the skull beneath the skin'.

It is not necessary for us to consider their lives or works in detail here but it would be immensely helpful if you were able to include them in a little private study and reading. Ben Jonson's incredible use of iambic pentameter would be a particularly interesting comparison for you to make, and Christopher Marlowe's life, ending in a tavern brawl and including accusations of being a spy, makes intriguing historical reading.

Most of Shakespeare's contemporaries were far better educated men and tended to look down upon the grammar school boy – although this was very likely to be caused by jealousy of his incredible success. The exception to this sneering attitude was Ben Jonson, who had great admiration for Shakespeare's work and is arguably the only writer who came close to challenging his excellence.

Shakespeare, like all other playwrights, is relying upon you to 'put his work across' and communicate it to a variety of recipients: he is the genius in the partnership but he is also dead and he is nothing without the actor's ability to bring his soul alive again through his work.

CONSPIRACY THEORIES

Many people believe that William Shakespeare did not actually write the plays that are attributed to him, and that the historical figure we recognize as him was actually a 'cover' figure, used to conceal the real identity of the writer. Indeed, some people believe this theory, in various forms, to the point of obsession and there have been many books written upon the subject, most of them advocating an alternative person as the real playwright. One of the most popular choices of these is Francis Bacon (there are many scholars who fervently believe the plays should be attributed to him), but there are also many other contenders. However, there are plenty of worthy academics who believe these theories to be ridiculous and no one has come anywhere near to proving that Shakespeare was not the author of the works.

For your purposes it is really not necessary for you to concern yourself with the validity of these conspiracy theories. After all, one thing is certain, the plays exist and nothing can dispute their importance and magnificence.

However, there is one aspect of the theories that may be worth noting and that is the reason for them. The argument is that the man historically identified as William Shakespeare could not have written the plays because he would almost certainly have lacked the education and experience to have done so. The plays are full of references to matters of high cultural and educational significance. The conspiracy theorists believe that their authorship would require a man with far greater knowledge of language, geography and cultural diversity and, perhaps more importantly, one who was of a higher class than

There are many Shakespearean detectives.

the only really important point is that Shakespeare exists; whether or not he is the man history thinks he is.

THE PLAYS

List A – Category

COMEDIES
All's Well That Ends Well
As You Like It
The Comedy of Errors
Love's Labour's Lost
Measure for Measure
The Merchant of Venice
The Merry Wives of Windsor
A Midsummer Night's Dream
Much Ado About Nothing
The Taming of the Shrew
The Tempest
Twelfth Night
Two Gentlemen of Verona
The Winter's Tale

HISTORIES
Cymbeline
Henry IV, Part I
Henry IV, Part II
Henry V
Henry VI, Part I
Henry VI, Part II
Henry VI, Part III
Henry VIII
King John
Pericles
Richard II
Richard III

Shakespeare, with greater experience of high living and aristocratic pursuits.

Whether or not, as a reason, this holds water is debatable, but it does highlight just how wonderfully rich, colourful and highly textured the plays are. Not only do they contain great stories with incredible insights into the human experience, but they are also wonderful resources of a vast array of information and cultural references. While the authenticity of much of this information has to be balanced with the fact that the plays are primarily works of fiction, this depth and complexity gives the actor an incredible wealth of source material. Therefore, perhaps

TRAGEDIES
Antony and Cleopatra
Coriolanus
Hamlet
Julius Caesar
King Lear
Macbeth
Othello
Romeo and Juliet
Timon of Athens
Titus Andronicus
Troilus and Cressida

List B – Best Estimated Chronology

PLAY	
Henry VI, Part I	1589–1590
Henry VI, Part II	1590–1591
Henry VI, Part III	1590–1591
Richard III	1592–1593
Two Gentlemen of Verona	1592–1594
The Taming of the Shrew	1593–1594
Titus Andronicus	1593–1594
The Comedy of Errors	1593–1594
Romeo and Juliet	1594–1596
The Merchant of Venice	1594–1597
Richard II	1595
Love's Labour's Lost	1595
King John	1595–1596
A Midsummer Night's Dream	1595–1596
Henry IV, Part I	1596–1597
The Merry Wives of Windsor	1597
Henry IV, Part II	1598
Henry V	1598–1599
Much Ado About Nothing	1598–1599
As You Like It	1599
Julius Caesar	1599
Hamlet	1600–1601
Troilus and Cressida	1600–1608
Twelfth Night	1601–1602
All's Well That Ends Well	1602–1603
Measure for Measure	1604
Othello	1604
King Lear	1605
Macbeth	1605–1606
Coriolanus	1607–1608
Antony and Cleopatra	1607–1608
Timon of Athens	1607–1608
Pericles	1607–1608
Cymbeline	1609–1610
The Winter's Tale	1610–1611
The Tempest	1611
Henry VIII	1612–1613

The last of the plays, *Two Noble Kinsmen*, has been left off the list as it was almost certainly mainly written by John Fletcher, Shakespeare's great friend and his successor as main playwright for the King's Men. Such is the intrigue of Shakespeare – but now the fun really begins!

2 INTERPRETATION

Kathryn Hunter as Richard III at Shakespeare's Globe Theatre in London, 2003. (Photo: Robbie Jack)

A BIASED VIEW

Many people are prejudiced against Shakespeare in one, or all, of three ways. Some simply do not like his work, finding it difficult, irrelevant and boring. Others do like the plays, either emphatically or, at the very least, they suspect that there might just be something of interest for them lurking amongst the pages but they believe the works to be far too 'worthy' and themselves far too unlearned to be able to appreciate them properly or even engage with them at all. A third sample of the population both like and, to differing degrees, understand and are attuned to Shakespeare but consider the actual performance of the plays a prob-lematical and, sometimes, unobtainable quest.

As you have decided to read this book it is to be assumed that you may fall into one of these categories of prejudice: possibly, but not neces-sarily, the third. On the other hand you may bridle at this, priding yourself on your open minded, balanced and informed approach to the Bard. However, despite this, you will be nonetheless anxious to lean how to improve your Shakespearean acting and it will be help-ful therefore for you to understand the prejudice in others and how it must be over-come.

As with all prejudice, the root of this partic-ular evil lies in fear and ignorance: each of these two interlopers feeding upon the other.

Shakespeare can be boring at school.

THE PROBLEM OF UNDERSTANDING

Prejudice aside, there can be very few of us (however enlightened and pro-Shakespeare we may be) who, on opening a Shakespearean text, are not sometimes confused and unclear as to the meaning and purpose of the words before us. As you will discover in this chapter, much of this difficulty is assumed, imagined and exaggerated and descrambling the information into vivid clarity is both easy and enjoyable. However, as a performer, it may be wise before progressing further to remind yourself just why you are anxious to undertake this task.

Yours is no selfish quest, for you are the champion of your audience: it is for their benefit that you pursue your studies for, unless you have a clear understanding of the play and its situations, you cannot hope to convey this to others. It must be remembered that an audience should not be principally involved in an academic exercise: they are there to enjoy a story and have clear and unhindered access to all of the various literary and artistic qualities that the play can afford them. Their digestion of these qualities may, arguably, be an academic exercise, but the basic receiving of story, meaning and intention is not. Indeed, while Shakespeare is undoubtedly laden with artistic worthiness, it is fundamentally and absolutely based upon storytelling and it is to this discipline that you, as performers, are most dedicated.

There is a massive clue here as to the way you should pursue your understanding of Shakespeare's plays: not in any sense from an academic or learned point of view, but rather as one simply unravelling stories of human life and endeavour.

The 'imagined' problem of understanding

Actually, Shakespeare is not difficult to understand at all – not really. While the works themselves are obviously great literary achievements, the actual text was not (and is not) intellectually demanding at all. Indeed, how could it be when a great percentage of Shakespeare's audiences were not intellectually or educationally developed in any way? It is ridiculous to suggest that what they could understand perfectly is now impenetrable to us just because a few hundred years have passed.

Neither can we fall back on the old myth that the plays were written in 'Old English' – they were not. The truth of the matter is that the use of language has changed somewhat over those years (but not nearly as much as we sometimes think), and society and its conventions and values has obviously changed too, though, again, not nearly as radically as may at first appear.

Understanding Shakespeare is simply a matter of accepting this and remembering to view the text not directly as we might a modern work, but from an angle: slightly off kilter, so to speak. When reading Shakespeare you must 'see' and not just 'look'; you must 'think' and not just 'assume'; you must allow your brain to recognize universal and timeless truths, rather than modern conceptions based upon how you see the world and use language.

If you are able to make this adjustment then what at first seemed coded and obscure, will suddenly be revealed as straightforward, clear and immediately accessible. Your job then will be to transmit and convey this to an audience in a way that will allow them to bypass the 'understanding process' and have direct contact with the text in all its simplicity: to afford them instant recognition of the myriad of basic human conditions and experiences for which Shakespeare is so richly famed.

So, rather than thinking of how you might 'understand' Shakespeare's works, you must think in terms of how to 'view' them in the right way and at the right 'angle'.

EASIER THAN YOU THINK

In order to explain the process properly (and allow you to see how easy it actually is) it will be a good idea to examine some specific examples of Shakespearean text and use them as illuminative to the process. However, before looking at these it is important that you remember two things:

* These examples are not chosen particularly for their ease or difficulty of understanding: they are just examples and the processes that you will be engaging in can be applied to any other part of Shakespeare's canon.
* When viewing the following text make it your rule that you will look for what is there and not what you think is there: do not make assumptions but simply open your mind and let the meaning become apparent to you without prejudice or preconditioning based upon how you perceive life and how you use language. In other words, look at these words with the eye of a human, any human, and not with the eye of a particular human in a particular country in this very particular twenty-first century.

EXERCISE – ENCOUNTERING VIOLA

So firstly, as an example of how the unusual nature of Shakespearean language can blind us to the very obvious, basic and incredibly

Happy actor!

accessible meaning that it contains, it will help you immensely to read the following speech of Viola's from *Twelfth Night*. It is presented here in two interwoven forms: Shakespeare's lines (in italics) are followed by a very basically unfettered version centred purely on the direct meaning. This will allow you to clearly observe how straightforward, down-to-earth and uncomplicated this speech really is.

It should be noted that this is not a translation as such but an attempt to recreate the essential gist of the character's intention and articulation. In fact, in order to make the point and point the meaning as graphically as possible, there is some embellishment and

Reading the Plays

When you need to read a complete Shakespeare play, or (even more importantly) you are rehearsing one, never use a Complete Works edition. You should certainly own one of these as they are extremely useful for reference and visiting small sections when required. However, the small print and seemingly endless columns of dense text can make them very daunting and off-putting for sustained reading and work. Many a would-be Shakespearian practitioner has been utterly deterred by such a depressing introduction to a play.

When focusing fully upon a particular title, buy or borrow an individual copy; with fewer but bigger words on each page: they are much more user friendly, and will provide a much happier experience.

The best editions to acquire are those with good and comprehensive notes and, even better, those with half a page of text with the relevant notes below on the same page. With this arrangement it is much easier to focus upon small pieces of the play at a time (with helpful information readily available) and not to become overwhelmed by the amount of text as a whole.

vulgarization. It is the essence of the speech that is our quest here. Neither has any attempt been made to follow each line in pattern of versification but just to recreate each section in broken prose roughly following the verse structure.

Obviously a prerequisite of understanding individual sections of a play is to have a prior knowledge of at least the story of the play itself. Therefore, if you are not acquainted with the plot of this play, take some time to locate and read a synopsis before you continue further. Having done this, the following will serve as a brief and very basic introduction to the speech itself and put it into some kind of context:

In the speech Viola, who is dressed and living as a boy (one of Shakespeare's favourite conventions), has just had a ring thrown at her by the angry servant of a lady to whom she has just delivered a message from her master whom she loves herself. The speech centres on her gradual (although not completely correct) realization that the key to her confusion about the situation (but not yours, hopefully) is her ridiculous, and now much regretted, disguise.

So to the speech itself:

Viola. *I left no ring with her; what means this lady?*
I didn't leave her a ring. What's she on about?
Fortune forbid my outside hath not charm'd her!
Don't tell me she fancies me!
She made good view of me; indeed, so much,
That sure methought her eyes had lost her tongue
She did keep staring at me all the time – and didn't say much...
For she did speak in starts distractedly.
...except a few stammered sentences that didn't make much sense.
She loves me, sure; the cunning of her passion
Invites me in this churlish messenger.
She's fallen in love with me and she trying to get my attention by a rude servant going on about some ring.
None of my lord's ring! Why, he sent her none.
'I don't want your Lord's ring'...he didn't send her one and she knows it.

I am the man: if it be so, as 'tis,
Poor lady, she were better love a dream.
I'm the one she fancies and if that's true (which it obviously is) the poor woman would be better off loving a fantasy figure in her imagination.
Disguise, I see, thou art a wickedness,
Pretending to be someone else is ridiculous.
Wherein the pregnant enemy does much.
It seems very exciting at first but there's always some disaster waiting to kick you where it hurts.
How easy is it for the proper-false
In women's waxen hearts to set their forms!
How easily we women fall in love with the first bloke that looks as if he can provide for our needs.
Alas! our frailty is the cause, not we!
Unfortunately it is our weakness that is the trouble.
For such as we are made of, such we be.
We just can't help being pathetic creatures (heavy irony).
How will this fadge?
What will happen here (how will it work out)?
My master loves her dearly;
My boss really loves this woman
And I, poor monster, fond as much on him;
and I, stupid fool that I am, love him just as much.
And she, mistaken, seems to dote on me.
On top of that she, getting it wrong, seems to fancy me like crazy.
As I am man,
Disguised as a man,
My state is desperate for my master's love;
It's hopeless my being in love with my boss because he thinks I'm a bloke;
As I am woman,
As the real girl that I am,

– now alas the day! –
Oh blimey
What thriftless sighs shall poor Olivia breathe!
Olivia's going to waste her time sighing and swooning over someone who's not equipped as she thinks.
O time! thou must untangle this, not I;
I'll just have to leave it to sort itself out eventually;
It is too hard a knot for me to untie.
I can't possibly sort it out myself.

A Closer Look

Hopefully, any mist surrounding this speech will now be beginning to clear, but to complete the process it will be useful to revisit some of the lines and observe why they mean what they do and why it might have been possible to

I left no ring with her!

either misinterpret them or not understand them at all. Once you have done this you will have well and truly started to equip yourself with a technique for demystifying any of Shakespeare's scenes.

Look first at the line: *Fortune forbid my outside hath not charm'd her!* It contains two very common Shakespearean elements. Firstly, an exclamation – *Fortune forbid*: in today's language we use many oaths, swear words and exclamations to punctuate our verbal communication. We are very used to these and toss them into our speech without too much care or significance. Rarely do we see them written down and their standing within language is that of a tool of emphasis and punctuation rather than meaning, even though we can usually trace some kind of logical link to their usage.

Because Shakespeare's exclamationary language (of which there is much) is broadly unfamiliar to us we can, if we are not careful, use it too literally or place too much emphasis upon its sound. Thus it becomes an encumbrance when, in fact, it is usually a great help and stimulus to naturalism and spontaneity when speaking the lines. *Fortune forbid* is a fairly straightforward example but later in the speech, *now alas the day,* is somewhat less familiar and more likely to cause the inexperienced student to over-emphasize it or give it disproportionate meaning.

Remember to look out for these tiny gems of language: they are there to help you and they can be used to really bring your verse speaking alive, but beware that they do not unduly 'muddy the waters' for you and cause you to become too involved in their literal meaning.

The rest of the line – *my outside hath not charm'd her!* – is a beautiful use of language.

There is great precision here as Viola references the fact that it is her outer image that has prompted the sexual attraction: this is picked up later in the speech when she rebukes womankind for too readily choosing a mate from outward appearance without waiting to discover the person that lies beneath it. It also adroitly underlines the predicament of Viola appearing to be something (or someone) she is not.

The words *charm'd her* refer, of course, to the beguiling effect that her 'outer image' has had upon her hostess. In fact, when we break the whole line down in this way its meaning is obvious but, nonetheless, it is couched in a way which would be unfamiliar with all but the most romantically-minded modern person. All that is needed here is for you to look at what is being said clearly, literally and with a mind to Shakespeare's mastery of poetic phrasing – then its meaning becomes crystal clear and all unfamiliarity falls away. The fact that Shakespeare has used his mastery of artistic and poetic language to actually reference several aspects of the situation here must not blind you to the simplicity of the literal statement of – *she fancies me!*

Now look at this very interesting line: *In women's waxen hearts to set their forms!*. The metaphor itself here is simple – a woman's heart (her love) can be easily determined upon an object of love (a man). However, the interesting aspect is the use of 'wax' within the metaphor: wax sets from its liquid form into a solid mass very quickly and securely (this is why it is used to seal documents). Thus, Shakespeare completes a very succinct image of 'the heart' committing and devoting itself within a very short time of being presented with an 'object' that it might desire.

The most important point to note in this example is that Shakespeare is using quite a subtle and complex device to state a very obvious thing. It might be reasonable to ask why he does this: if his lines are really so simple, why does he seemingly over complicate them? (This has certainly been the cry of many a schoolchild over the years.) The answer is two-fold: firstly, there is so much beauty in the language – this image is, in itself, both intriguing and enchanting; secondly, the poetic nature of the image allows more depth of meaning to be conveyed – the point is made more roundly and fully and far more personally to the listener than mere practical and direct prose could ever hope to achieve. The cumulative effect of this rich and poetical imagery, line by line, is to provide the audience or reader with an extraordinary layered approach to meaning that enlightens and informs way beyond hard and basic facts.

However, as you have seen, at the very root of each line are very straightforward and universally recognisable intentions and truths. It is these that the actor must identify and with which she or he must work. This identification is not nearly as hard as it seems and the rich and colourful language (and, as you will see in a later chapter, the verse) helps the work, not hinders it.

EXERCISE – TRY FOR YOURSELF

In order to begin to improve your confidence in the understanding of the works you aim to perform, follow the following exercise:

* Carefully read the speech that follows these instructions. It is one of Puck's monologues from A *Midsummer Night's Dream* and, as such, is broadly suitable for both male and female actors.
* Then read the synopsis of the speech's basic meaning and story that follows it. This basically details what Puck is saying in the speech but, although it makes general reference to some of the metaphors used, it does not specifically provide a line-by-line commentary or any illumination of a particular word or phrases.
* Read the speech again and now try to supply your own understanding of each line. Remember to open your mind and not to make any quick assumptions. Keep

Good notes can illuminate a text.

reading each section in the context of the meaning of the whole speech and do not allow yourself to be sidetracked by jumping too quickly upon the seemingly obvious: let the speech reveal itself to you slowly rather than trying to 'shake' the meaning out of it.

My mistress with a monster is in love.
Near to her close and consecrated bower,
While she was in her dull and sleeping hour,
A crew of patches, rude mechanicals,
That work for bread upon Athenian stalls,
Were met together to rehearse a play,
Intended for great Theseus' nuptial-day.
The shallowest thick-skin of that barren sort,
Who Pyramus presented in their sport
Forsook his scene and entered in a brake:
When I did him at this advantage take,
An ass's nole I fixed on his head:

Anon his Thisbe must be answered,
And forth my mimic comes. When they him
    spy,
As wild geese that the creeping fowler eye,
Or russet-pated choughs, many in sort,
Rising and cawing at the guns report,
Sever themselves and madly sweep the sky,
So at his sight, away his fellows fly;
And, at our stamp, here o'er and o'er one falls;
He murder cries, and help from Athens calls.
Their sense, thus weak, lost with their fears
    thus strong,
Made senseless things begin to do them
    wrong;
For briers an thorns at their apparel snatch;
Some sleeves, some hats, from yielders all
    things catch.
I led them on in this distracted fear,
And left sweet Pyramus translated there:

When in that moment, so it came to pass,
Titania waked, and straightway loved an ass.

The Story

Puck (a fairy) is reporting to his boss, Oberon (King of the Fairies), about a successful trick he has played upon Titania (Queen of the Fairies) at Oberon's request. He tells him that she is now in love with a 'monster'. He states that, while she was asleep, a group of working class men were rehearsing a play (for presentation at a royal wedding) nearby. Puck has a low and comical opinion of these men. He has singled out the most stupid of them (in his opinion) a character called Bottom who is playing Pyramus in the play, and, while away

My mistress with a monster is in love!

from the others (perhaps answering a call of nature) he has turned his head in to that of a donkey's. On seeing this, Bottom's fellow actors flee in terror, believing him to be a monster. Puck chases after them himself and, because they are too frantically escaping to even look round, they assume that the monster is 'hard on their heels'. They, stumble, fall and end up in total disarray – much to Puck's amusement. In the meantime, Titania wakes up, sees the absurd image of Bottom and, because Puck has previously cast an ingenious spell upon her, instantly falls in love with him. Puck tells all of this to Oberon with much self-congratulatory relish and fun.

After the Exercise

When, and only when, you have completed your own investigation of Puck's speech, it may be helpful and interesting for you to consider the following few points of interest regarding meaning and understanding. Compare these to your own interpretation and see how you initially responded to them.

The word 'close' in the second line of the speech refers to the area being closely confined (small) not near to – this is a classic example of how you can be misled if you are not careful. The word 'consecrated' is also interesting here because it does not refer to an actual religious consecration (as of a church for example) but uses the core meaning of the word (to set apart for sacred purpose) and thus, indirectly, gives a strong feeling of specialness to the character of Titania: this is hugely economical and shows how poetic language can really say so much with so few words.

'Who Pyramus presented' in line nine looks a little confusing at first but it simply means that Bottom was playing Pyramus in their play ('their sport', as Puck puts it, with perhaps a little irony). A reader's confusion here simply stems from the fact that the phrase is constructed back to front from a modern standpoint but still makes perfect grammatical sense if you think about it.

'Anon his Thisbe must be answered' in line thirteen is another beautiful use of economic language but can be a little complex. Thisbe is the female character that Bottom is playing opposite (thus 'his' Thisbe) and this simply means that Bottom must return to the rehearsal because it is his turn to speak (his colleague playing Thisbe has given him his cue).

'Sever themselves and madly sweep the sky' in line eighteen may be a little problematic, but this is another fine example of Shakespeare stating a simple fact in an extraordinary and beguiling way. You will know that to sever means to part or divide but it may be difficult to see how it applies here – until you realize that these metaphorical birds are 'parting and dividing' themselves from each other and from the ground, as they fly madly up into the sky with an explosion of movement. This is not a use of language that is unfamiliar to us because of time differences but simply because of its amazing clever and succinct approach to simple meaning and storytelling.

The phrase 'from yielders all things catch' at the end of line twenty-five presents you with a very fine use and choice of one particular word – yielders. This word, with one particular meaning based around giving up, resigning and surrendering, is a marvellous way of summing up the plight of these poor men and somehow really compounds the image of their terrified and chaotic flight from 'horrendous danger'.

'And left sweet Pyramus translated there' is close to the end of the speech in line twenty-seven. This is not particularly difficult to understand but it should be noticed that Shakespeare chooses to use the word 'translated' rather than 'changed'. It seems to be a better word to choose, but you have to be careful that you do not initially read it (and examples like it) and focus immediately upon its most common form of modern usage – 'to translate language': it is in these brief moments of assumption that the snowballing effect of confusion and misinterpretation can begin with all their quite unnecessary resulting problems.

EXERCISE – A GENTLE PERFORMANCE

By now you should have a good working understanding of Puck's wonderful speech. Now it is time for you to use this knowledge for the purpose that it is intended – to bring the speech off the page and into life. Remember you are not an academic; you have studied this speech for the sole purpose of being able to perform it in a clear and entertaining way.

So now read the speech out loud several times and experiment with your understanding of it. Do not pressurize yourself – this is not meant to be a full rendition with complete characterization, but just a way of gently discovering the sort of direction your understanding of the lines may take you in. You will by now know the story of the speech, or at least have your own interpretation of what is being said, so just simply tell the story, bring the words alive and inform your audience – albeit your own reflection in the mirror or your bedroom wall.

Handy Hint 6

Know What It Means – to You

One of the fundamental rules of acting is that you cannot act something properly if you do not know what it means. However, the precision of your understanding is not perhaps as vital as you may think. In order to make a line convincing, truthful and believable you must not be vague in any way about why you are saying it; but, provided it is clear to you what it means, it is not necessarily a disaster if you have misinterpreted its original meaning slightly.

An actor must make sense of the work they are presenting. An interpretation may not be exactly in accordance with the playwright's thinking but, provided it makes sense in context and is consistent throughout the play, it will do its job.

Naturally, you should be as accurate as you can be with meaning, otherwise the play will stray from its intentions, but it is better to have a clear thought that is slightly wrong than attempt to act a line with no thought at all.

THE OTHER SIDE OF INTERPRETATION

As an actor, with the fundamental purpose of giving the Shakespearian texts life away from the page, an understanding of meaning and intention within the lines is the first priority upon your interpretation skills – it is the 'grass roots' fundamental of your thinking about the play and the role you are playing. However, there is, of course, a great deal more to interpretation than this alone: once you have established the foundations in this way, next comes the task of interpreting the themes, purposes and philosophies of the play, along with an interpretation of your character and his or her place within the overall scheme of the work.

The good news is that here lies the most enjoyable and fascinating of tasks. Knowing what the lines actually mean is the first step upon a wonderful journey of discovery, which will lead you toward your goal of allowing an audience access to the most incredible plays ever written. As you move onwards in your study of performing Shakespeare, you will realize this more and more, and what may have at one time seemed daunting will translate into a challenge that you are able to meet with great skill and pleasure.

Interpretation liberates the actor.

3 AN ACTOR'S APPRECIATION

Dominic West (Orlando), Sienna Miller (Celia) and
Helen McCrory (Rosalind) in As You Like It at
Wyndhams Theatre, London, 2005. (Photo: Robbie Jack)

THE ACTOR AFRAID

Many actors are frightened of Shakespeare – or, at least, they think they are. They see this particular playwright as one best to be avoided or, if they are serious about acting and understand that the greatest exponent of their chosen art form cannot really be avoided, they approach him with fear, trepidation or, at best, acute suspicion. When asked why this is, most are unable to supply a reasoned answer. Instead they submit a conglomeration of the kind of prejudices, preconceptions and misunderstandings that were discussed in the previous chapter.

Further probing will usually reveal that their fears are similar to those of a child who convinces themselves that a Bogey Man lurks menacingly behind the wardrobe of their darkened bedrooms: it is a fear of the unknown, exacerbated by an equally awesome dread of turning on the light and investigating. Some actors simply refuse to illuminate and face their fears, preferring to stick doggedly to their belief that Shakespeare is 'not for them'. This is a great pity for, if they were to only 'stiffen the sinews and summon up the blood' just a little, they would not only discover their concerns were imaginary but that, far from being a Bogey Man, Shakespeare is much more like a benevolent uncle, intent on helping them to fulfil the potential of their talents.

Ironically, it is the lesser playwrights who

Many actors are afraid of Shakespeare.

should cause an actor concern, particularly the 'very lesser' ones; for it is a solid truth of the dramatic arts that the less skilled a playwright is, the harder they are to act. An inept author will not provide the immediate advantages of depth of character, wealth of ideas and subtleties of plot and situation that are the great enablers of the actor. Instead,

---

Handy Hint 7

Read Some Good Plays

As well as reading Shakespeare, you should also build and encourage your understanding of the benefits that good dramatic literature can offer an actor as well as an audience, by steadily building your knowledge of works by other great playwrights and institutions – from all periods.

Thankfully, your choice in this regard is vast, but some vaguely organized suggestions of some juicy reading or investigation are: Sophocles (Greek), Seneca (Roman), Mystery Plays (Medieval), Commedia (Italian Renaissance), Christopher Marlowe, Ben Jonson, John Webster, Congreve, Dryden, Sheridan, Goldsmith, Wilde, Shaw, Ibsen, Chekhov, Pirandello, Noel Coward, Arthur Miller, Tennessee Williams, Eugene O'Neill, Brecht, Fry, Pinter, Wesker, Shaffer, Beckett, Ionesco, Dario Fo, Edward Bond, Alan Ayckbourn, Edward Albee, Alan Bennett, Michael Frayn, Tom Stoppard, Willy Russell, John Godber, David Rudkin, Peter Flannery, Sarah Daniels, Jim Cartwright, Steven Berkoff, Caryl Churchill.

Do not approach this task by reading the entire works of each playwright in turn, but 'dip in' here and there and gradually enhance your knowledge using the list as a guide. This should be a happy, long-term task and not a chore.

---

two-dimensional characterizations, lack of any real dramatic content and dreary storylines prove to be the greatest of disablers – forcing the actor to rely far more upon his or her own resources and skills to compensate. As with most areas of life, the better the materials, the better the job.

Although Shakespeare is not beloved by quite the entire population of the theatre community, his genius as a playwright is beyond doubt. An actor should not allow fear to negate this and inhibit a cautious, if not total, embracing of his talent enhancing properties. There can be no doubt that Shakespeare helps one to act well: he is an indispensable aid to good acting.

In order to understand why so many actors do not trust this vital theory, it may be useful to examine, as far as it is possible, what exactly constitutes good acting and what bad. It will be even more helpful to do this with reference to how Shakespeare and a bad playwright may contribute to these respectively. Not, it must be quickly stressed, that these two poles of excellence and ineptitude exist without much variance of ability between them; but that it will serve good purpose to consider the detrimental effects of extreme awfulness in order to appreciate the enhancing effects of the absolute opposite.

THE ACTOR IN DISGRACE

A bad actor is one who lacks believability and truth; whose characterizations are not convincing; who speaks the text without spontaneity; who appears physically 'wooden' and uncoordinated; who fails to give the written words they have learned a life liberated from the page; who fails to convince that they are living the lives of their fictitious creations forwards – from moment to moment; who cannot present complexity of ideas; who cannot be convincing and moving emotionally; and, above all, who cannot naturally facilitate the myriad of communication devices used by a human being when thought and action are perfectly harnessed and in the right order. Or to put it another way, a bad actor does not 'think the text' but merely regurgitates it with resulting lack of naturalness. Without doubt this list could be easily developed and extended but it will suffice for now.

A bad playwright encourages and strengthens the bad habits of a bad actor by failing to supply the stimulus they require. It is extremely difficult for an actor to appear real and convincing if the character she or he is attempting to portray is stereotypical and superficial: text that is trite, stilted, hackneyed or poorly constructed is considerably difficult to translate into natural, free-flowing and communicable thoughts; badly paced plot and unbalanced emotional content find an actor struggling to live effectively from moment to moment in the scene – with cracks in the construction of the play becoming easily apparent in the performance of the actor; it is much harder for an actor to appear comfortable, relaxed and in control of their performance when they are trying to inhabit a poorly drawn personality in a totally unbelievable world, far from the audience's recognition.

The plain fact that bad plays are harder to act must not, however, be used as an excuse: for it is here that the actor really earns her or his crust and where their skills are most desperately needed. But what joy and relief can ensue when a playwright's skills are complementary to the process and work with, rather

Actors in disgrace!

than against, the actor – nurturing, encouraging and enabling a fine performance with so much less angst.

THE ACTOR IN GLORY

A good actor is one who, obviously enough, is the opposite of the creature described before. However, good acting is more than just the positive alternative to a long list of negative points, and a good actor is more than just one who is in possession of all that a bad actor doesn't have and without those poor habits that he does. A good actor is one who can take a piece of literature and literally breathe life into it and recreate it from the page to the stage. Good acting is about effectively turning life back up the right way for the audience: taking something that already exists in writing and making it appear new, fresh, immediate and, above all, natural. This simply cannot be done without spontaneity, coordination, truth, integrity, control of body and voice or the simple but vital ability to put the thought before the word.

It is in the pages of a Shakespearean text that can be found so much fuel that is needed to drive fine and proper acting. Firstly there is a great wealth of ideas, feeling and emotions for the actor to feast upon – Shakespeare having the quite remarkable ability to explore vividly so many of the traits, vulnerabilities, concerns, preoccupations, passions, fears and desires that constitute the human soul. However, this is not, by far, the end of the story: his plays are constructed using the most deep and beautiful language which, if allowed, will flow freely and effortlessly into meaningful thought and communication. His plots are perfectly paced and balanced – allowing the actor to move convincingly along a character's timeline; his verse is so immaculately constructed that it will almost lift the actor and carry them along their path of truth within the play. His characters are fully formed, multi-dimensional, interesting, complex and human – a joy to play, never a chore. The themes within the plays are strong and well founded, giving the actor a strong and vital backbone to their work on the text. And, as examined in the previous chapter, Shakespeare's plays are, contrary to popular belief, straightforward, accessible and direct – illuminating a clear and safe path for the actor to follow.

All of this is not to say that performing

Actors in glory!

Shakespeare is easy – if this were so it would not be worth studying and you would not be reading this book. However, it is certainly easier to approach and master than you may have grown to believe and, without doubt, the plays are far more serviceable than many of the potboilers one might embrace more readily.

EXERCISE – IDENTIFYING THE POSITIVE

To begin your Shakespearean performing voyage of discovery in earnest now, attempt the following exercise.

Handy Hint 8

Learn From Other Actors

One of the best ways to improve your Shakespearean performing ability is to watch other actors as often as you can. You will find that the best of them have the unfailing ability to make the job look surprisingly easy. Text that may have seemed to you impenetrable will suddenly spring to life with amazing clarity when handled by a true expert. As you watch, you will see how a combination of clear thinking and technical dexterity allows the actors really to liberate the words from the page in a startlingly colourful and dynamic way.

By the same token, a bad Shakespearean actor can be illuminating too, by virtue of showing how easy it is to get things wrong. Try to identify mistakes as you see them but do not dwell on these performances. Seek out the best and watch them avidly.

Read through this short speech, using a set of notes to make sure that you understand it in reasonable detail. It is from Act IV, scene i, of *The Tempest* and is spoken by Ariel, who has brought the drunken conspirators, Stephano and Trinculo, to be punished by Prospero.

I told you, sir, they were red-hot with drinking;
So fun of valour that they smote the air
For breathing in their faces; beat the ground
For kissing of their feet; yet always bending
Towards their project. Then I beat my tabour;
At which, like unback'd colts, they prick'd their
ears,
Advanced their eyelids, lifted up their noses
As they smelt music: so I charm'd their ears
That calf-like they my lowing follow'd through

Tooth'd briers, sharp furzes, pricking goss and
thorns,
Which entered their frail shins: at last I left them
I' the filthy-mantled pool beyond your cell,
There dancing up to the chins, that the foul lake
O'erstunk their feet.

On a piece of paper, make notes concerning all the parts of this speech where you think Shakespeare is being particularly clever or effective in his use of language. That is, where he gives an astute insight into either the character or the situation by a skilled use of imagery and construction. Look out for metaphors, juxtapositions between words, and vivid descriptive phrases. Try also to angle your appraisal towards performance. In other words, attempt to identify areas of particular aid and interest to the actor as well as purely literary merits.

This is, of course, a very personal exercise, and your notes will almost certainly vary from those of another actor. This fact is, in itself, indicative of the depth of quality that Shakespeare presents.

Now look at the same speech again below with some 'appreciative' notes appended to lines throughout. You might not agree with them and your notes may be quite different, but reading them should start you thinking in the right way about the text if you are not already doing so.

I told you, sir, they were red-hot with drinking;

This is a very simple but directly effective image for drunkenness – also implying guilt.

So fun of valour that they smote the air
For breathing in their faces; beat the ground

Drunken behaviour is common in Shakespearean scenes.

Their pumped-up bravery is wonderfully delineated by this reference to being aggressive towards the very elements themselves. It also gives a strong image for the actor to demonstrate physically if wished.

For kissing of their feet; yet always bending
Towards their project. Then I beat my tabour;

A very clever development and enhancing of the previous image.

At which, like unback'd colts, they prick'd their
    ears,
Advanced their eyelids, lifted up their noses
As they smelt music: so I charm'd their ears

A strong reference to Ariel's skill in 'charming' them, and one that the actor can use to really underpin the character. There is fine and supporting rhythm to this too.

That calf-like they my lowing follow'd through

This is a tremendous metaphor – cleverly presented in two parts (that connect perfectly) by stressing the way in which they (calf-like) followed him (his 'lowing').

Tooth'd briers, sharp furzes, pricking goss and
    thorns,
Which entered their frail shins: at last I left them

The superiority of Shakespeare's sprites.

*Always keep notes of
your work.*

A very fine image of their journey – emphasizing their enchantment and drunkenness simultaneously.

> *I' the filthy-mantled pool beyond your cell,*
> *There dancing up to the chins, that the foul lake*
> *O'erstunk their feet.*

This finale gives the actor a marvellous opportunity to show the implicit superiority the character feels about these human unfortunates.

Complete this exercise by picking your own example of a short piece of text from another play, and see how many positive points and observations you can make of it.

Handy Hint 9

Keep Notes

As you progress through the chapters of this book, it will help you to make notes about your studies and to document your progress. If you are working properly you will find yourself often having moments of illumination, when you suddenly realize how to do something or perceive that something you thought difficult is actually becoming quite easy. Don't let these 'eureka' moments slip from your mind – write them down for future reference and encouragement.

It will be particularly helpful for you to document your progress through the various exercises. This will allow you to see how you develop each time you attempt (or re-attempt) one.

When you start to work with other people in exercise and rehearsal situations, a diary-type record of your work will really enable you to see development and progression.

4   A Shakespearean Voice

David Calder (Lear) and Jodie McNee (Cordelia) in King Lear *at Shakespeare's Globe Theatre, London. (Photo: Robbie Jack)*

Vocal Skills

One of the most common pitfalls faced by an actor is the danger of placing too much emphasis upon the words that they speak and the voice they use to speak them. When working with a written medium, as actors do, it is often all too easy to focus considerable attention upon the audible elements of the performance, while relatively ignoring the visual and, sometimes, the cerebral. This is equally true of Shakespearean work as it is of any other, in fact more so, as the truly wondrous nature of Shakespeare's poetry and his literary genius positively encourages such an imbalance to exist: the Shakespearean actor can forget quicker than any other that he or she possesses a body and a brain as well as a voice.

However, having established this, and with a firm resolve to redress the problem with equal emphasis and study of movement and interpretation, it cannot be denied that Shakespearean acting places severe demands upon an actor's vocal skills.

It is also true that the Shakespearean actor must possess a 'good voice' but, sadly, the definition of a 'good voice' is often misinterpreted. Shakespearean acting is much associated with rich and fruity tones, soaring cadenzas of speech and elegant purity of pronunciation. These images probably have more to do with the past than they do with the present and can be disheartening for an actor with a less impressive vocal instrument than some of the practitioners of old. This is not to say that quality of voice is not admirable and desirable, but that it is not the only, or indeed the most important, factor in determining a good Shakespearean voice. Therefore, those who consider their voices of a more ordinary nature, while they should always work towards improvement, should not be put off.

The truly important vocal skills that must be acquired, developed and honed are those of strength, accuracy, dexterity, variety and, above all, flexibility. All of these are well within the capabilities of all actors to achieve, and

Handy Hint 10

Love Your Voice

One of the most often used pieces of self-criticism by actors is disliking their voice. This is due to the simple fact that individuals do not personally hear their own voice in the same way that others hear it. As well as hearing through the ears in the normal way, it is heard internally as well, thus giving a false impression as to its tone and resonance. Therefore, when the voice is heard recorded it sounds very different and comparatively thinner and less full in quality. In most cases this is a false impression created by the unfamiliarity of the sound.

The problem is that you do not usually hear your voice in this way very often and, therefore, do not have the opportunity to get used to it. Then, when you do hear it recorded, your brain rejects and dislikes it.

It will be counterproductive for you to have this negative view of your voice from the outset, and you must learn to love your voice – for it is a unique and intrinsically expressive part of the being that is 'you'. In order to achieve this, listen to your recorded voice as much as possible and, instead of criticizing it, enjoy it and note its beauty and strengths. Then, as you continue to work and develop it, keep listening to it and monitor the improvements to the sound.

Strength, accuracy, dexterity and variety.

ion, while also being able to control and utilize this breath on its outward journey into speech. Nothing makes more demands upon the excellence of breath control than one of Shakespeare's plays. Not only does the work call upon a wide range of technical and emotional vocal variety – all of which must be powered and supported by the breath – but the demands of the verse-speaking, in particular, make the ability to harness and utilize this breath of vital importance.

THE INWARD BREATH

Breath constitutes power and energy for the actor – not only vocally but, often, emotionally as well. Therefore, an actor needs to ensure that her or his breathing is deep and full. However, it is of utmost importance that this is achieved naturally, spontaneously and without causing tension – for tension is the enemy of all actors and will completely negate the advantages that deep breathing presents.

In everyday life most people breathe reasonably shallowly but are usually used to, and quite capable of, taking a deep breath when required – indeed, modern existence requires this as a restorative from time to time. However, in order to achieve the automatic and intuitive nature of such breathing, the Shakespearean actor must practise deep breathing in a systematic way and this can be best achieved by including the inward breath in their exercise routine.

There are many such exercises, designed to promote and foster a good breathing technique, and it is a good idea to experiment with a variety of these from the large array of sources available. However, the exercises in this chapter will make an excellent starting

systematically improve, and studying them is infinitely more encouraging than dreaming of attaining a sonorous voice to rival grandees of theatrical history.

TO BREATHE OR NOT TO BREATHE

There are many vital ingredients to developing a vocal instrument equal to the task of amplifying a Shakespearean text effectively, but all of them start and end with their most important constituent – the breath. A Shakespearean actor must be able to breathe fully and deeply, but also in a totally relaxed and intuitive fash-

point and a very firm basis for regular practice. It is important to note that 'regular' is the important word here for, as with all exercise regimes, little and often is of far greater use than lots occasionally.

WHAT HAPPENS WHEN WE BREATHE

Before commencing breathing exercises, it is necessary for you to have a very rough picture in your mind of what occurs within your body as you breathe. This may sound obvious, as it is well known that we breathe into our lungs,

In a tight space, don't breathe in – breathe out!

but we are not always aware of how this is achieved.

The body possesses muscles that form a duplex of breathing apparatus. These are the ribs and the diaphragm and, working together, they have an effect very similar to bellows: sucking air in and then blowing it out again.

As we inhale, our ribs expand (the first 'bellows' effect), pulling the air in. As this happens, room is created within the body for the diaphragm to drop downward (the second 'bellows' effect). This pulls more air inwards. The exact reverse occurs when we breathe out: the diaphragm pulls upwards, pushing air out, and then the ribs do likewise by descending.

Thus this process of inhaling has the effect of expanding the body – breathing makes us bigger. This is not always the common conception of breathing as many believe that breathing, because it is something of a sucking action, makes us smaller (you may have heard the cry of 'breathe in' as people enter a small and confined space, such as a crowded elevator).

For your purposes it is essential that you focus upon the concept of becoming bigger as you inhale deeply. Think not only of creating space for as much breath as possible, but also of your 'acting being' becoming larger, fuller, more generous, more expansive, and more energetic. All acting is about the utilization of human energy and Shakespeare, in particular, requires this energy in abundance: breath is the very 'fuel' that drives this 'engine'.

Because of the different size and nature of the two main pieces of breathing apparatus, the diaphragm tends to produce quicker, more muscular and dynamic exhalations, while the ribs steadier, longer and more measured ones.

EXERCISE – DEEP BREATHING (1)

Stand with your feet shoulder width apart, your feet turned out slightly, your knees slightly flexed, your back comfortably straight and feel a relaxed openness across your chest. Foster and enjoy the feeling of being tall, firm and physically and emotionally powerful.

Gently push air out of your body through your mouth firmly until you are quite empty. Hold this empty state for a time until you feel the instinctive need to breathe.

Allow an inward breath to start: this should feel as if you are relaxing the hold upon your breath and the resulting inhalation is automatic and natural.

Continue the inward breath until you are comfortably full. As this happens monitor the amount of expansion that is occurring in the upper part of your body as your ribs expand and your diaphragm drops down (you will be aware of this by your tummy being displaced and moving forwards), and relish the ease with which this expansion takes place.

Hold this full breath for a few seconds and, during this time, feel an increased sense of power and dynamism in your body and mind as this energy and life-giving force inhabits you.

While holding the breath, also check that your neck and shoulders have remained relaxed – roll them slightly if this helps to dispel any tension that may have appeared. Particularly make sure that the inward breath

Monitor the movement of ribs and diaphragm.

Open up the ribs.

has not caused your shoulders to rise up – it is the ribs that should move when breathing in deeply, not the shoulders as is commonly believed.

Push the breath firmly outwards again in a slow, steady stream, making sure that your exhalation is reasonably even and steady. Continue to gently push outwards until you are completely empty once more.

Allow the next inward breath to start. This now should really feel an automatic response – that you are 'allowing' something to happen rather than 'making' something happen. However, be careful not to gasp the air in as if in a panic response – keep the intake smooth and controlled.

When you are full again, hold the breath for a few seconds and note the further increased expansion from the previous breath. This should not feel forced, though – you should feel relaxed, in control and strong. Imagine the breath as pure energy, naturally inhabiting you and ready to be used, not only for dynamic speaking but dynamic acting too.

Begin to push the air out through your mouth again and continue the cycle of this exercise for around six repetitions.

This exercise can make one feel giddy and light-headed, especially when practised for the first time. If you experience this, stop immediately.

In order to really experience the expansion of your ribs, it might be helpful to undertake this exercise again in a different position.

Lunge forward so that one foot is placed in front of the other and then swing your hands up in front of you with elbows bent. This will create a rounded back and, as you breathe, you will feel your ribs open and expand.

EXERCISE – DEEP BREATHING (2)

Expelling your entire breath first, take a long full inhalation as in the previous exercise and hold this still for a few seconds. This time, instead of slowly exhaling in a constant stream, push the air outwards in a shorter, more powerful manner – this should feel like a strong, energetic 'pant' that expels the intake quickly and forcibly.

At the end of the short 'pant' breathe in again as quickly and as fully as possible.

Expel the breath again in the same way as before and repeat this process of 'panting' for around thirty repetitions. Keep each exhalation and inhalation sharp, firm and energetic – but do not rush or 'snatch' at them – control is always of paramount importance.

As you undertake this exercise you should notice that the outward breath, because of its 'panting' nature, is powered more by the diaphragm than the ribs. In fact, you may find that the ribs only lower a little on each exhalation, leaving the diaphragm to do the hard work and retaining a fair amount of expansion and fullness for the duration of the exercise. This is very good, as it allows the body to top up quickly and efficiently while retaining a certain 'reserve' of breath at all times. You should be aware of this happening and foster the feeling of control and power that gives you, as the demands of Shakespearean verse-speaking requires a good deal of breath control and stamina.

Once again, make sure as you undertake this exercise that you do not become light-headed or hyperventilate. If in doubt – stop!

EXERCISE – DEEP BREATHING (3)

Repeat the previous exercise but, this time, replace the silent outward 'pant' breath with the sound 'Bah': this is the vowel sound in the words 'bath', 'laugh' and 'car' with a 'B' in front of it.

Do not try to make the sound too loud but do keep it firm, muscular and dynamic: think about the strength and energy of the sound as you make it.

After ten repetitions of this audible 'pant', change the sound to 'Boo': this is the vowel sound in the words 'food', 'loo' and 'stew' again with a 'B' fronting it. Make a further ten repetitions.

Keep changing the sound each ten repetitions in the following cycle:

Bah
Boo
Bee – the sound as in 'teeth', 'sea' and 'key'
Bay – the sound as in 'lay', 'day' and 'pay'
Boh – the sound as in 'low', 'show' and 'flow'
Bi – the sound as in 'fly', 'pie' and 'sky'
Ber – the sound as in 'heard', 'nurse' and 'verse'
Bow – the sound as in 'now', 'bough' and 'cow'.

The making of these sounds will, of course, require your lips, tongue and jaw to move too, so make sure that these movements are equally as precise and energized as your breathing.

Repeat this cycle (ten repetitions each) six more times but each new cycle of sounds should now be fronted by a different consonant each time. Having started with 'B' you should now move through 'D', 'P', 'L' and 'W' in the following full sequence:

Dah, Doo, Dee, Day, Doh, Di, Der, Dow
Pah, Poo, Pee, Pay, Poh, Pi, Per, Pow
Lah, Loo, Lee, Lay, Loh, Li, Ler, Low
Wah, Woo, Wee, Way, Woh, Wi, Wer, Wow.

Finally, return once more to the original sequence of Bah, Boo, Bee, Bay, Boh, Bi, Ber, Bow.

Control Is Everything

While it is vitally important for the Shakespearean actor to breathe fully and deeply, this accomplishment is of little use in terms of speaking the text if the outward breath cannot be controlled.

For the actor, breath equates to power: proper breathing enables the voice to be tonally rich and engaging and the 'support' given to the voice, as it sits upon an upward force of air, enables it to carry audibly and clearly through the acting space without recourse to straining and thinning of the tone.

Control is the final factor in this equation and, when performing Shakespeare, it is certainly the most important. You will discover just how important when you begin to work upon your verse-speaking skills. One of the most vital factors is that breath is controlled instinctively and without too much conscious thought: breathing and its usage are vital but the content of the text requires much cerebral agility and there is little room at the front of the actor's conscious brain for guiding the technical mechanics of the vocal process.

For this reason an automatic resourcefulness of control must be developed and, to this end, the following exercises should be considered as extremely important.

Exercise – Breath Control (1)

Expel all breath and then fill up fully as in the previous exercises.

Form an 'S' sound with the tip of your tongue against the back of your top teeth (like the sound of escaping gas) and push the breath out through this sound to the mental count of ten (approximately ten seconds). Be careful to ensure that the sound is steady throughout without any wavering – you will need to push the sound fairly firmly to achieve this without, of course, letting this run you out of breath before 'ten'. Also make sure that you do not 'dump' too much breath when you start – keep control from the outset and make the whole exhalation smooth and equal. You should not attempt to have breath left at the end of the count but, rather, be just comfortably empty without straining through the final few seconds. As the process happens, be aware of your diaphragm pulling up (you will feel this as your tummy pulling in) your ribs slowly and smoothly descending. It is this feeling that engenders the control.

As you complete the count, allow your body to fill with air again in the same full and deep way that you will by now be used to. Repeat the process for three repetitions.

Now go straight on to a further three repetitions but, this time replace the 'S' sound with a hum. This can be of any pitch but make sure that it is a note that sits comfortably in your register so that you can place the sound forward upon your lips – you should feel them tingle slightly. Again, it is vitally important that the sound remains steady and constant throughout the count and that you apportion the outward breath reasonably equally so that you are just empty again by 'ten'. Remember that this whole exercise is about control and keep your mind focused upon this fact while you are working.

There should now follow a final three repetitions, this time using an 'Ah' sound – the sound in the word 'car'. In order to place this sound as far forward as possible and to avoid a harsh 'glottal shock', start the exhalation with a 'hum' as before and then, as you reach the count of 'two' let your jaw drop open into the

Feel the hum tingle.

sound. It should be noted here that 'Ah' is the most open of all the vowel sounds and, therefore, you should let your mouth open as wide as possible without forcing: do not try to control the sound by limiting the space by which it can escape, but let your breathing muscles do all the work. The large open space of the mouth makes the process harder than before.

The complete nine repetitions of this exercise can be particularly taxing when you are not used to this level of breathing and control, so do be careful.

EXERCISE – BREATH CONTROL (2)

Speak the following lines of simple dialogue, breathing only at the end of each line where marked. Try to keep your voice steady and smooth as you speak and use the whole of each breath evenly through the line. You will see that each line gets a little longer than the one before – so be ready for this. Also, try to ensure that your voice remains natural and responsive throughout – speak it normally and not as a robot would.

I don't think I'll go in holiday this year [breath].
I've had so many expenses lately that I can't afford it [breath].
Not that I don't need one but you can't have what you can't pay for [breath].
I'll probably just have a few days down at Uncle Philip's caravan instead [breath].

Repeat the four lines and, this time, make sure that you are not taking any sneaky breaths during the lines – this can happen without your being aware of it if you are not careful.

Complete a further four repetitions (six in all).

Open the jaw for the sound 'Ah'.

EXERCISE – BREATH CONTROL (3)

Now attempt the same process but this time you will find that the breath points are marked in various locations and not necessarily at the end of the line. It is important for the sake of the exercise that you only take a breath where marked. This means that you will need to be particularly careful to keep to the instructions and not instinctively breathe when you want to.

I'm sorry to bother you [breath] *but I just noticed you from across the street and I simply had to come over and ask you something.* [breath] *I've been looking for a coat like yours for simply ages but I haven't been able to get one anywhere.* [breath] *I hope you don't mind me asking where you got yours from because* [breath] *it's just what I want.* [breath] *They're so warm, these types of coats, aren't they?* [breath] *I can't imagine why all the shops don't sell them but you wouldn't believe the trouble I've had finding a place that does.*

This last exercise, as well as continuing to develop your breath control, begins to heighten your awareness of the relationship between breathing and emphasis within a dramatic text – particularly a classical one. For example the breath indicator before '*it's just what I want*', while slightly unusual in its location, tends to lead the speaker to an excited, exclamatory rendition of the phrase. Likewise, the lack of breathing pauses in the long last sentence can create a feeling of 'gabbling' excitement. It is vital to explore this relationship between both technical and interpretational requirements, as the two are inextricably entwined in acting generally but particularly when it comes to verse speaking.

EXERCISE – BREATH CONTROL (4)

Take your usual first long, full breath. Count aloud the number 'one' – then fill up again.

Now count 'one', 'two' – and then fill up. Now count 'one', 'two', 'three' – and then fill up. Continue in this way, adding a number each time, until you reach 'twenty'.

This is a deceptively simple exercise but there are two factors to be careful of. Firstly, do not just let your breath spill out on the early, easy counts – consciously make sure that your outward breath is fully under control and the sound remains supported and thus full in tone (not breathy or thin – neither overly loud or emphatic). Secondly, the last few counts (especially the very last) are quite long for one breath. Therefore, resist the temptation to rush or 'snatch' at the sounds – keep the count steady and at the same pace and intensity as the shorter ones. You should be aiming to feel the same degree of technical dexterity and control each time you speak, whatever the length or difficulty of the phrase. This exercise, like the others, is designed to develop an instinctive and automatic vocal ability that will serve you in all situations and leave your conscious mind more space for the real business of interpretation and characterization.

Handy Hint 11

Practice

It is an unshakable fact that, in order to become proficient at anything, one must practise regularly. The exercises in this chapter, and those in the rest of the book, will only be of use to you if you partake of them regularly. They may be varied, added to and adapted, but they must be part of an ongoing and disciplined routine if they are to be effective.

Many people make the mistake of working hard and long at an exercise or exercises, forget all about them for ages, and then wonder why they see no improvement. Little and often is the key to progress. Exercise is repetitive by its very nature and if you work too long at it you will become stale and bored. It is far better to construct an exercise regime which you can move swiftly but thoroughly through and then use it at least three times a week or daily if possible.

Remember also to use the vocal exercises (and the physical ones later in the book) as warm-ups for all of your text-based work. This will not only focus and enliven you, but will also make sure that you do no damage when going at the acting full pelt.

Remember too, that of all the theatrical disciplines, voice is the one which requires most exercise work in order to achieve any results at all, let alone significant ones. However, do not let this put you off – if you work hard you will definitely see the benefits before too long.

'VARIETY IS THE SPICE OF LIFE'

Even a very limited study of speaking for the theatre will reveal the importance of the words 'pitch, pace and pause', and the associated importance of the word 'variety'. When young children begin to take speech and drama lessons they invariably soon find themselves involved in the development of varied approaches to these main elements of speech and, if they continue with the subject, this continues throughout their lives. In a very bald and basic way, variety of pitch, pace and pause is the very stuff of effective speaking.

For your purposes here, it is probably best to separate the three in the sense that pace and pause, while they can be studied in their own rights, are intrinsically part of the interpretational process of acting rather than directly technical. However, pitch is a different matter, being an element of vocalizing that can be directly related to quality of voice rather than usage. Singers are very well aware of the importance of developing and stretching the range of their voices and often concentrate upon this by way of specific exercises away from their working repertoire. Actors should approach the subject in the same way, as an extensive range and variety of notes in their voice is a prime technical requirement for tackling the demands of challenging texts.

Nowhere is this truer than in the case of Shakespeare's plays. Shakespeare peppers his work with a spectacular display of literary 'fireworks', full of beautiful and complex words and phrasing. His use of language is spectacularly rich, diverse and exotic. This places huge demands upon all aspects of an actor's voice but it is easy to overlook or underestimate the importance of vocal range.

It is difficult to examine variety of pitch without reference to the associated vocal elements of 'colour' and 'tone'. It has already been established that you do not need to possess a wondrously beautiful and melodious

voice in order to act Shakespeare. However, it is important to make the most of the voice that you have (whatever quality you may consider it to be) and while it is impossible for you to exchange your voice for another, it is possible for you to develop, extend, improve and enrich the one that you have.

The soaring, splendid, elegant and evocative language found in a Shakespeare play must be matched with a palate of notes, colours and tones worthy of, and equal to, the job of liberating them from the page and doing them justice upon the stage. It may well be that you do not like your voice (very few people like the sound of their own voice) and have doubts that it is 'up to the job'. You must dispel these negative and unwarranted thoughts immediately, for you will be truly surprised just how easy it is for you to improve the variety, tonality and musicality of your voice – with some work!

EXERCISE – VOCAL QUALITY AND PITCH (1)

Gently hum a note that is reasonably low in your register but one that is comfortable and you can support and project without it becoming 'gravelly' or dropping back into your throat.

Having established the note – take a full breath in the way you have been practising and hum the note for a mental count of ten (approximately ten seconds). Keep the sound forward on your lips and try to feel its reverberation in the mask of your face. When the count is complete, fill up with breath as usual.

Now repeat the hum, again to the mental count of ten, but this time move up to the next note in the scale. Continue to repeat this process until you have completed the octave.

Speak musically.

Finally, continue repeating the exercise, but this time moving back down the octave step by step.

Throughout this exercise it is absolutely vital to keep the hum forward in the face and 'buzzy'. If you let it drop back into your body you will wreck, rather than improve, the tone. If you find this difficult to achieve, you may find that you have started too low in your register and need to start a little higher. It is also important not to forget your breath control just because you are now focusing upon a different vocal discipline – as you hum each note through the count, keep the exhalation steady.

If you find the exercise difficult to pitch, enlist the help of a piano or keyboard – experiment to find your starting note and then work up the scale from there.

EXERCISE – VOCAL QUALITY AND PITCH (2)

Remembering to breathe properly from the start, find your starting note from the previous exercise and sing it using a 'Mah' sound – this is the very open sound as in the word 'jar' with an 'm' placed before it. Remember to open your mouth wide as the jaw drops open. As you are mid-note, let your voice soar up in pitch to the same note but an octave above, then let the note drop back down again in steps (singing each note separately) to return to the original note. All of this must be accomplished on one breath and with the sound forward and free.

Now hum up one note of the scale and use this as your new starting point. Repeat the process as before, rising to the octave above and then stepping back down in one breath. This time, of course, your highest note point will be one note higher in the scale than before.

Keep repeating the exercise and each time start another note upwards on the scale, until you feel that the highest note is only just comfortable for you – push this as far as you dare, but make sure that you do not strain or hurt your voice in any way. With practice, you should find that your register slowly but surely increases.

Return to your original starting note (the one comfortably lowest in your register) and start the whole exercise again only, this time, using the sound 'Moo' – the sound in the word 'two' with the same 'm' in front. Complete the exercise to your comfortably highest note as before.

Complete the exercise two further times changing the sound to 'May' and 'Me' respectively – these sound as the words they spell. Use the consonant 'm' to gently push your voice forwards prior to the mouth opening into the vowel sound – remember the tingle.

While this exercise is ideally suited to your purposes it is in essence a singing exercise. Do not let this put you off, especially if you consider yourself a poor singer. How you sound musically is not important: it is the quality of tone and range of pitch that you need to be concerned with.

A simple keyboard will aid practice.

Also, you may find even greater need for the aid of a keyboard, either electric or acoustic. It should be easy for you to find your starting note and finishing note but, if you want to play along each descending note in the scale to prompt you vocally and you are not a pianist (each scale will employ different black notes), try enlisting the help of a friend with more musical knowledge.

EXERCISE – VOCAL QUALITY AND PITCH (3)

Speak the following Shakespearean sonnet, letting your speaking voice find as many different notes in the process as possible. Artificially soar upwards and downwards in your range, utilizing as many different qualities of pitch as you can. Allow some words or phrases to drop low, lift others high and experiment with all of the notes in between. It will sound over-exalted, unnatural and even silly: do not worry about this – just remember not to push the highs and lows further than feels comfortable and fully supportable with breath. You can find a particular 'free range' to your register in the last two lines, as the rhyming couplet just lends itself to excessive musicality of speaking.

> *Music to hear, why hear'st thou music sadly?*
> *Sweets with sweets war not, joy delights in joy.*
> *Why lov'st thou that which thou receiv'st not*
> *   gladly,*
> *Or else receiv'st with pleasure thine annoy?*
> *If the true concord of well tuned sounds,*
> *By unions married, do offend thine ear,*
> *They do but sweetly chide thee, who confounds*
> *In singleness the parts that thou shouldst bear.*
> *Mark how one string, sweet husband to another,*
> *Strikes each in each by mutual ordering;*

> *Resembling sire, and child, and happy mother,*
> *Who all in one, one pleasing note do sing;*
> *Whose speechless song, being many, seeming one,*
> *Sings this to thee, 'Thou single wilt prove none.'*

Now apply the same artificially wide-ranging pitch dynamics to this beautifully extravagant speech from Act II, scene ii, of Shakespeare's play *Antony and Cleopatra*. Although the speaker, Enobarbus, is very obviously a man, the speech will prove equally suitable for female actors in the context of this exercise.

> *The barge she sat in, like a burnished throne*
> *Burned on the water. The poop was beaten gold;*
> *Purple the sails, and so perfumed that*
> *The winds were love-sick with them. The oars*
> *Were silver,*
> *Which to the tune of flutes kept stroke, and made*
> *The water which they beat to follow faster,*
> *As amorous of their strokes. For her own person,*
> *It beggared all description. She did lie*
> *In her pavilion – cloth of gold, of tissue –*
> *O'er-picturing that Venus where we see*
> *The fancy outwork nature. On each side her*
> *Stood pretty dimpled boys, like smiling Cupids,*
> *With divers-colored fans whose wind did seem*
> *To glow the delicate cheeks which they did cool,*
> *And what they undid did.*

Finally, for this exercise, repeat the speech, this time without recourse to such exaggerated variation of pitch. However, let your voice rise and fall in a natural way and experiment with how many notes you can utilize in your voice in order to convey the colour and feeling of the piece truthfully and without artifice.

The final element of this exercise is particularly important. You may well be surprised at how liberated and flexible the tone and pitch of your voice can be. Repeat the exercise regularly and use alternative texts of your own choosing if you wish: the range and texture of your speaking voice should improve apace.

When working upon this and other speeches, make sure that you understand what you are saying – even in the artificially varied element. A good set of notes for the play in question will help you enormously in this respect and should always be used for this and all other text exercises.

ARTICULATION, ARTICULATION, ARTICULATION

There can be absolutely no doubt that Shakespearean texts contain an abundance of words in every conceivable variety of length, construction and meaning. It is equally undeniable that their density, complexity and rapidity require extremely precise speaking, based upon most arduous articulation.

Hamlet's words *'Speak the speech, I pray you, as I pronounced it to you, trippingly on the tongue'* could and should be interpreted as a direct warning to you, his 'players', as to the dangers of sloppy diction. A good set of notes will tell you that 'trippingly' means nimbly and fluently and these are excellent watchwords for the Shakespearean actor. Not only must your speaking be accurate but it must also be energetic and dynamic, able to dance over the text without losing any the subtleties of sound and content.

The very process of articulation itself can present a danger: while concentrating upon the precise pronunciation of the words it is all too easy to become laboured and stilted. The competent Shakespearean voice should be able to glide through and 'ride' the text: making clear each element of its construction while not becoming 'bogged down', stagnant and heavy.

With this in mind, you must pay considerable attention to the workings of your tongue, lips and jaw if you are to develop a sufficiently dextrous technique of diction. Remember that the workings of day-to-day speech do not generally tax the diction too roundly – even for those who are intent on maintaining clear and precise communication; modern plays require a little more work and concentration for their amplification and projection to an audience; but the classics, and Shakespeare in particular, are a wholly different matter and working upon them vocally, without proper preparation, can be something of a humbling experience.

These factors are by way of an honest warning and not intended to dishearten or discourage: quite the reverse in fact, for some good solid vocal work will enable you to make immensely accessible, fascinating and enjoyable that which, without such labours, would be difficult and unrewarding.

The first of the following exercises will show you just how difficult the demands of Shakespearean articulation can be and those that follow will greatly help you in acquiring the 'tools' of diction needed to be more than adequately equal to the challenge.

EXERCISE – ARTICULATION (1)

Read out loud the following prose speech from Act II, scene ii, of *Hamlet* at a moderate pace.

You are welcome, masters, welcome, all. I am glad to see thee well. Welcome, good friends. O, old friend, why, thy face is valanced since I saw thee last. Com'st thou to beard me in Denmark? What, my young lady and mistress? By'r Lady, your ladyship is nearer to heaven than when I saw you last by the altitude of a chopine. Pray God your voice, like a piece of uncurrent gold, be not cracked within the ring. – Masters, you are all welcome. We'll e'en to't like French falconers, fly at anything we see. We'll have a speech straight. Come, give us a taste of your quality. Come, a passionate speech.

You will experience various difficulties, not only in relation to the density and rapidity of the language but especially here in terms of the many apostrophized words, which are very common in Shakespeare's plays. These tend to increase the number of consonants in relation to vowels in the speech and thus strain the articulation further.

If, by any chance, you did not find the articulation of the speech challenging, increase your speaking pace until you can feel the limits of your consonantal prowess.

In order to experience a similar challenge, but this time, with verse-speaking thrown into the mix, speak aloud this speech of Joan La Pucelle's from Act V, scene iv, of *Henry the Sixth, Part 1*. Like the male speeches used for these voice exercises, it is quite usable by either sex for these purposes.

First, let me tell you whom you have condemn'd:
Not me begotten of a shepherd swain,
But issued from the progeny of Kings;
Virtuous and holy; chosen from above,
By inspiration of celestial grace,
To work exceeding miracles on earth.
I never had to do with wicked spirits;
But you, that are polluted with your lusts,
Stain'd with the guiltless blood of innocents,

Corrupt and tainted with a thousand vices,
Because you want the grace that others have,
You judge it straight a thing impossible
To compass wonders but by help of devils.
No, misconceived! Joan of Arc hath been
A virgin from her tender infancy,
Chaste and immaculate in very thought;
Whose maiden blood, thus rigorously effused,
Will cry for vengeance at the gates of heaven.

One of the main features of difficulty here is the variety, rapidity and juxtaposition of the consonantal sounds – placing a considerable emphasis upon the dexterity of lips and tongue.

This exercise should be spoken 'cold' without pre-study. However, after your initial attempts, employ some notes to facilitate a good understanding of the speeches: never see, touch, speak or breathe any Shakespeare without endeavouring to demystify it – whatever the exercise may be.

EXERCISE – ARTICULATION (2)

Using the Tongue

Using your hands, stroke your jaw open, so that your mouth is wide but in a relaxed way with your lower jaw simply hanging loose. There should be at least a two-finger gap between your teeth. Place the tip of your tongue just behind the upper teeth (it will have to stretch very slightly if the mouth is nice and wide) and then pull it sharply away to make a 't' sound. Make sure that this sound is crisp and sharp and not breathy – a quick precise 'tap'.

At a moderate pace and a steady rhythm, make ten of these sounds consecutively like this: t – t – t – t – t – t – t – t – t – t. Keep the sound percussively sharp at all times.

Repeat the ten 'taps' but this time voice the sounds a 'da' (the sound as in dirt) in this way: da – da – da – da – da – da – da – da – da – da. Do not allow too much air to escape and keep the sound firm.

Now return to the 't' sound and repeat the ten taps but this time at double the previous speed. This should sound a little like a machine gun but keep the sound steady and make sure that each 't' is clean and distinct. As long as your first rendition wasn't too fast you should be able to control it at twice the speed without too much difficulty.

Do the same with 'da' – doubling the speed in the same way.

Repeat the whole exercise so far three times – like this:

Steady beat: t – t – t – t – t – t – t – t – t – t
Double speed: t–t–t–t–t–t–t–t–t
Steady beat: da – da – da – da – da – da – da – da – da – da
Double speed: da-da-da-da-da-da-da-da-da-da.

EXERCISE – ARTICULATION (3)

Using the Lips
Warm up your lips by pushing them forwards into a pout, and then pulling them back pursed. Repeat this several times, increasing the speed each time. Now speak the following

Stretch those tongues!

sequence of sounds, very slowly, making sure that the lips come together firmly and precisely:

mar-me, may-me, moh-me, moo-me

Repeat these sounds in a round, gradually building the speed until this is quite fast.

Next, speak the following sequences of sound – again, starting slowly and then increasing speed gradually to fast:

me, me, me, me, me, me, me, me, me, me, me, me, me, me,
may, may, may, may, may, may, may, may, may, may, may, may, may, may,
my, my, my, my, my, my, my, my, my, my, my, my, my, my,
mum, mum, mum, mum, mum, mum, mum, mum, mum, mum, mum, mum,

EXERCISE – ARTICULATION (4)

Begin by relaxing your jaw – stroke it down with your hands and let it hang loose. Speak the following sequence of sounds – very slowly and carefully.

many men, many men, many men, men, men, many men, many men, many men, men, men, many men, many men, many men, men, men, many men, many men, men, men.

Repeat it in a round and gradually build the speed each time. Become faster and faster but stop when you can no longer maintain clarity and accuracy of speech.

Handy Hint 12

Tone Through Articulation

Tone and resonance of voice is usually thought of in terms of vowel sounds, but articulation plays a strong part here too. Let the tone of your voice flow into the consonants, particularly at the ends of words, as if the resonance of your voice permeates each word and fills up every corner and space within it. Enjoy the precision of your articulation and take pleasure in making the words sound full and sumptuous. Try not to make a distinction between what you are doing technically and what you are doing artistically – use the sounds of the words to express the meaning and aim to demonstrate the twin and parallel virtues of clarity of thought and clarity of word.

If you really carefully watch some of the great Shakespearean actors on film, and concentrate for a while upon their mouths, you will see not only a crispness of diction but also a sensitivity and beauty in the shapes that their lips make as they relish the words that they are saying – try to emulate this as, it is a wonderful shortcut to encouraging your performances to be fascinating and compelling.

To finish – try to sing the words instead of speaking them. You will find that they will fit perfectly to the tune of the *William Tell* Overture. Increase the speed as before and continue until you lose crispness and detail. Have fun with this exercise – it makes a good company warm-up when working with others.

5   THE WONDER OF VERSE

Jonathan Cake (Coriolanus) and Mo Sesay (Aufidius)
in Coriolanus *at the Globe Theatre in London, 2006.*
(Photo: Robbie Jack)

SHAKESPEARE'S WRITING

The purpose of this chapter is to introduce, analyse and experiment with Shakespearean verse-speaking, but before starting this process it will be helpful to remember that not all of Shakespeare's plays are written in verse all of the time.

Very often Shakespeare writes using a prose form: that is a normal writing style, utilizing sentences and standard punctuation in the usual way as common in most (but not all) modern plays. It is interesting to note that he will often employ this style of writing when conveying the more mundane down-to-earth aspect of his plots and he gives prose speeches to the characters tending towards a more straightforward and less emotionally charged nature.

For example, in the comedy *Much Ado About Nothing*, the principal characters of Beatrice and Benedick speak mainly in prose. Shakespeare has good reason for this as his choice of writing form underlines the pair's outward reluctance to show romantic and passionate inclinations. They scorn the frivolity and 'poetry' of the lover in favour of a more sensible and practical demeanour. Benedick, in particular, is a soldier, a 'man's man' with a steadfast, 'no nonsense' approach to life and his fellow men: therefore, the vaulting, artistic, elaborate tone of verse is quite inappropriate for him.

In the same play, the character of Hero, a far more imaginative, romantic and energized personality, speaks in verse with abandon. Thus it can be seen that even in the very choice of writing form itself, Shakespeare is able to inform and condition us to the nature of those who people his wonderful stories.

Hero and Beatrice are as different as verse and prose.

SHAKESPEARE'S VERSE

Firstly it is well to be sure of a reasonable definition of the term 'verse' in order to distinguish it from prose. Verse is certainly easy to recognize upon the page as the words are shaped and arranged into patterns. The sense within these patterns may often flow from one line to another and the ending of one line and the beginning of another is often dependent upon rhythm rather than sense. The rhythm of the writing is more pronounced than prose and, while sometimes gentle and subtle, can often be heavily underpinned by a regular pattern of stressed and unstressed syllables forming what is known as metre.

Probably of equal importance in dramatic terms is the way in which verse deals with and communicates language and its meanings. While prose will follow a logical sequence and grammatical order, verse can ignore these if necessary and present its truths in a more abstract and less ordered way: it can omit words, play with the rules of punctuation and make more use of figures of speech such as similes and metaphors. Thus verse can be truly 'poetic' and ignore the logical and literal in favour of the implied, alluded to and symbolic.

Verse form is a perfect dramatic vehicle in terms of the poetry of drama, and in Shakespeare's hands it becomes an inspirational tool for conveying character, meaning, situation and truth.

RHYMING COUPLETS

Sometimes the verse used by Shakespeare is paired into rhyming couplets (two lines of rhythmical association whose endings rhyme with each other). These are used quite sparingly but are all the more effective for this. Their use is often the opposite to that of prose, highlighting the most romantic, high-flown and exalted happenings and characters. For instance the highly romanticized and effervescent ending to *A Midsummer Night's Dream* is heavily littered with them: the play's emphasis is upon the ethereal and supernatural, making it an ideal depository for exuberant verse anyway.

THE SHAKESPEAREAN SONNET

Shakespeare's sonnets are a separate body of work from his plays and, therefore, are not of principal concern to you in your study here.

However, there is a uniformity, rhythmical purity and simplicity to their construction that make them an ideal starting point for the aspiring Shakespearean verse-speaker. For this reason, it is wise to include them in the body of work for this chapter and a sonnet will form the first practical exercise.

Shakespeare's sonnets are constructed using fourteen lines, divided into four recognizable sections. The first two sections form an octave (eight lines) formed of two quatrains (four lines), each with a rhyming pattern which runs *abab*: in other words the endings of alternate lines rhyme. The second two sections make a sestet, formed this time of another quatrain, rhyming in the same way, but followed by a final rhyming couplet with both line endings rhyming *aa*.

By using more of the alphabet, a sonnet can be most easily noted down identifying its rhyming pattern in the following way:

a, b, a, b, – first quatrain
c, d, c, d, – second quatrain
e, f, e, f, – third quatrain
g, g, – final couplet.

It is the final couplet that gives the sonnet its distinctive appearance and sound. The structure is designed to present an argument, to develop or perhaps contradict it and then, finally, to conclude it perfectly with a strong closing statement in the final couplet.

These sonnets are incredibly economic, self-contained poetic encapsulations and, although Shakespeare's verse in the plays is often less structured and more intellectually complex, the sonnets are fully indicative of his ability to be both poetic and meaningfully concise at the same time. Indeed, the sonnet form does appear within the plays sometimes any-way – as you will discover.

THE IAMBIC PENTAMETER

Shakespeare's principal and most used verse form, and the one with which you will be most concerned in your endeavours, is the iambic pentameter. It is this construction that runs freely and liberally through his plays and is the very bedrock and foundation of both his drama and an actor's performance of it.

To understand exactly what iambic pen-tameter is can be best achieved by looking at both words separately. Iambic refers to an *iambus* or an *iambic foot*. A 'foot' in this context is a section of metre, rather like a 'bar' in music. An iambic foot is one in which there are two beats, the second of which is stressed or given slight emphasis. Thus the two beats manifest themselves as: weak-**strong** or de-**dum.**

The word pentameter refers to the number of metrical feet in each line of the verse. More specifically, it indicates that there are five such feet. Therefore, iambic pentameter consists of five metrical feet of two syllables each, the sec-ond of which is stressed.

Shakespearean verse is perhaps more com-monly referred to as *blank verse*. This simply points to the fact that the iambic pentameter does not rhyme – it is 'blank'.

All Good Rules Have Exceptions

Examination of any length of Shakespearean verse text will quickly reveal that the iambic pentameter is not uniformly strictly adhered to. There are lines which certainly fit the prescribed format perfectly right down to the last syllable, but this is by no means constant: there are many lines that are a beat short or a beat too long and it is this 'variation' of the rule which helps to give the verse its colour, momentum and exciting unpredictability.

In the same way there are also exceptions to the 'blank' rule, the tool of rhyme being employed spasmodically and appropriately when required.

BE NOT AFRAID

Hopefully, these clinical explanations of Shakespeare's writing conventions will not have triggered or increased any anxiety within you. It is certainly true that acting in verse can seem, to many actors, a daunting practice and this is quite understandable. One of the con-tributory factors to this problem is our culture's increasing journey away from com-plexity and elegance of language and towards a greater and greater use of colloquial, pedes-trian, parochial and economic speaking. Television, with its capacity for, and propen-sity towards, naturalism and simplification, has played its part in this, encouraging and underlining a 'minimal effort' approach to language and communication and a watering-down of cultural excellence. This is not to say that television, and other modern media, have not produced some remarkable advances in both the arts and entertainment but, with such heavy soap operas and reality programming, it is little wonder that much of the populace feels even further removed from the language and disciplines of the classics.

However, as with most elements of Shakespeare, the problems are, for the most part, illusory and prejudicative. The first step in conquering a fear of verse-speaking is to attain a sense of perspective. It may be helpful to remember that Shakespeare was in many ways providing his audiences with contemporary fare, very similar in concept to the televisual sensations of today. Many of his customers were common people in search of escapism and fun, and it is very likely that much of what we see as high art in his language today would seem equally colloquial, pedestrian, parochial and economic then.

You must assure yourself at this stage that the seeming difficulties associated with the text of Shakespeare's plays are the result of unfamiliarity more than lack of relevant expertise. Familiarity is easy to obtain for those willing to commit a little effort to the process, and the remaining expertise required is readily obtainable with similar determination. It would be an over-simplification to say that speaking Shakespearean verse is 'easier than you think' but it is certainly far more accessible and workable than may appear to the nervous uninitiated.

The most important factor in the conquering of any fear is, as often is the case with Shakespeare, a startling revelation that you may at first find difficult to accept and embrace. It is that the Shakespeare's verse actually assists the acting process and facilitates the communication of meaning and feeling in a quite unique and liberating way.

In order to begin your journey from 'verse victim' to convert and advocate, you may begin by undertaking the following exercise.

EXERCISE – VERSE-SPEAKING (1)

Read slowly through the following sonnet; just read in your head at this stage and not aloud. Observe the way in which the unique rhythm and rhyming structure is formed and works.

To me, fair friend, you never can be old,
For as you were when first your eye I eyed,
Such seems your beauty still. Three winters cold
Have from the forests shook three summers pride,
Three beauteous springs to yellow autumn turned
In process of the seasons have I seen,
Three April perfumes in three hot Junes burned,
Since first I saw you fresh, which yet are green.
Ah, yet doth beauty, like a dial hand,
Steal from his figure, and no pace perceived;
So your sweet hue, which methinks still doth
    stand,
Hath motion, and mine eye may be deceived;
For fear of which, hear this, thou age unbred:
Ere you were born was beauty's summer dear.

Next, make sure, as always, that you understand basically what the poem is saying and the general meanings of each line. This understanding need not necessarily be academically accurate; more important is that you have an understanding of what it means to you and that you are not working in a vacuum and dealing with lines that are without personal relevance.

Now speak the sonnet aloud – clearly and slowly – and pay attention to the following factors.

✳ Use the rhyming structure as both structure and guide to your speaking. Aim for each rhyme and, when you arrive upon it,

THE WONDER OF VERSE

emphasize it slightly. Do not labour it or 'hammer' it but gently acknowledge it with your voice before passing on. This will allow you to find the implicit framework that is there in the poem: you can almost consider the rhymes as resting places with manageable areas of speakable words between.

* Think about your breathing. Keep it deep and full, and control it so that you do not lose it all between breaths – allowing you to top-up rather than completely inhale each time. Take a breath only at each punctuation mark. By doing this you not only begin to find fluidity but you will become used to differing lengths of phrasing and related breathing. Instances such as speaking just the word 'Ah' on one breath in the ninth line will allow you to pause as long as you wish (or as long as seems artistically appropriate) and then continue, letting the flow of the piece resume and the intrinsic rhythm automatically reassert itself without hindering the natural progression forwards through the lines.

* Be aware of the very obvious discrepancy between the end of line three and the fact that the sense of the sentence continues into line four and beyond. This is called an enjambment. In order to make this work you will need to experiment with the technique of suspensory pausing.

ENJAMBMENT AND THE SUSPENSORY PAUSE

There are many places within Shakespearean verse where the sense of something that is being said flows past and through a line ending and on to the next line – an enjambment.

This makes it difficult to execute a metrical pause – one at the end of a line, taken quite naturally, in order to facilitate the rhythm – without breaking the sense or causing it to become unwarrantedly jerky. However, to ignore the line end altogether breaks the rhythm and destroys the musicality of the verse.

The answer to this problem is the suspensory pause. When executing such a pause the last word of the line is suspended by pitch, length or both – the word is literally 'suspended' before moving on to the next word in the following line. Obviously, this must be achieved without taking a breath as might be possible in an ordinary metrical pause situation. In this way a sense of pausing is created without there being an actual 'gap' in the sound. Thus, the rhythm is preserved and the sense is properly served.

Practise this technique by repeating the last exercise and concentrating upon the enjambment between lines three and four.

THE SONG REMAINS THE SAME

One of the fundamental skills associated with verse-speaking is the ability to identify the implicit tune beneath the words. All good verse-speakers can hear this tune in their heads all the time they are speaking the words with their mouths. The nature of this tune is, of course, heavily dominated by rhythm, but present too is an unmistakable melodic framework, perpetrated by the rising and falling cadences and gentle musicality.

It is essentially important to realize that the verse-speaker does not need to emphasize this tune but simply to be aware of it. Indeed, one of the great dangers of verse-speaking is that

Handy Hint 13

Embrace the Enjambments

It may seem to you that an enjambment occurring in the verse is a nuisance, because it requires you to become adept at suspensory pausing. However, this is far from the case: in fact the reverse is true.

Suspensory pausing is actually quite a natural phenomenon. This is because, if you are aware of both the sense of what you are saying and the intrinsic rhythm and musicality of how you are saying it, you will find this type of pausing becomes almost automatic and instinctive. Once you are aware of this you will find that the ebb and flow of this type of pause positively adds to the musicality of your verse-speaking. It also allows you to create emphasis and emotional structure out of the very rhythm of the lines and words themselves.

You will find that your verse-speaking will start to have a natural 'swing' to it: not a habitual or didactic one; but a gentle one, allowing itself to be pulled and manipulated as the sense of the verse progresses.

the tune becomes over-pronounced and becomes too dominant, leading to a 'sing songy' style of delivery. However, of equal danger is that the song may be ignored and lost, eradicated in the speaker's desire to make sense of the text, and that the verse is transmuted into something more like prose.

In terms of Shakespearean verse-speaking, it is of immense help that one is working with the product of genius. The quality of versification and poetry is such that the 'tune' almost demands to be acknowledged and heard and, to this end, it will, to a certain extent, look after itself – becoming difficult to ignore and hard to negate.

Once an ability to 'hear the song' of the verse constantly throughout its speaking has become instinctive and habitual, the speaker may then begin to 'play' with the words, sounds, sub-rhythms, beats, syllables, inflections and pauses within it or, perhaps more accurately, on top of it: the song is there, organically and assuredly beneath, while atop it the speaker employs full range of artistic and technical variation and interpretation. The most significant aspect of this phenomenon is that the tune of the verse is always the boss, setting the rules and policing their adherence: for, although it bestows great freedom upon the speaker, granting considerable licence of implementation and usage, it remains the overall point of authority and standardization.

It should be emphasized at this point that, while the melodic qualities of verse should be encouraged rather than hidden, the rhythm must not be emphatic but rather ever-presently underlying and foundational. However, it must also be regarded as the principal structure of the verse and thus it must not be violated or desecrated in pursuit of acting and interpretation. That is not to say that acting and interpretation are not the most important factors when speaking Shakespeare – of course, they are – but they must be so 'because' of the verse rhythms and not 'despite' of them and, particularly, not at the expense of them. If the rhythm is stretched by pause, emphasis or variation, then this must be compensated for and adjusted later in the metre – if not the acting remains but the verse is lost and the acting is much the poorer for it.

This ability to make adjustments and maintain an ongoing relationship with rhythm while utilizing a full range of interpretational devices must be automatic and instinctive: it must not be over-conscious or laboured. This is why 'hearing' the tune, while never 'singing' it, is so important as you speak the words and interpret the meaning: the tune must be ever-present in your mind and soul whatever else is occupying your attention from moment to moment as you act the text.

THE EXAMPLE OF JAZZ

One of the best ways to understand the process working with the tune as foundation and structure to your speaking is to examine the similarities that exist in the playing and singing of jazz music.

When jazz musicians improvise they do so freely and imaginatively but they do so around the tune and the rhythm that they, and their fellow musicians, are playing. They pull and manipulate the musical lines, inspirationally utilizing changes of pace and pause. They often run notes together, jump octaves and flow along scales between main melody notes, but as they pull and manipulate the tune in this way, they are careful to continually hold the rhythm and reference the tune by compensating and balancing the bars as they go along.

It is probably more pertinently helpful for Shakespearean actors to consider this jazz analogy in terms of 'scat' singing – the vocal version of improvisational music. In vocal jazz, scat singing is vocal improvization with nonsense words and syllables or even without words at all. Scat gives singers the ability to sing improvized melodies and rhythms, to create the equivalent of an instrumental solo using their voice. While actors are certainly

using words that are definitely not nonsensical ones, the parallel of freely and inventively placing meandering vocal sounds around a structural tune is a good one: actors will, of course, place and meander meaning and interpretation around the tune too.

A key factor for any jazz musician is continually 'hearing the tune' – keeping the basic structure within awareness so that the extemporal elements of their playing or singing do not become undisciplined and thus falter. So too then must the Shakespearean actor and verse-speaker continually 'hear the tune' in much the same way and for the same reasons. This is obviously easier to achieve for the musician, for they will most likely have a band of fellow musicians playing the tune behind them – most significant of these being the rhythm section of bass and drums. The actor does not possess this luxury and so the tune must play within their heads, reliably keeping them within the disciplines of the verse being spoken.

However, this cerebral tune must not be too strong or overpowering for the musicality of verse, unlike music sometimes, is subtle and subconsciously persuasive.

It is this ability of an actor being aware and instinctively working with the musicality of Shakespearean lines that marks him or her out as an accomplished verse-speaker. It is not a skill than can be learned overnight, and you must be prepared for some considerable practice in order to acquire it initially and then develop it. However, it is well within the grasp of anyone who can speak and desires to communicate the Bard's work, and so you should not feel daunted by the task but relish the opportunity to engage with such a fascinating form of acting.

EXERCISE – VERSE-SPEAKING (2)

Hearing The Tune

Read the following piece of iambic pentameter verse from *Henry the Fifth*, Act III, scene i, in your head and not, at this stage, out loud. It is part of the wonderfully theatrical and rousing speech of Henry to his troops, and is full of both dynamic musicality and dramatic meaning. At this stage, try just to get an overall feel of its rhythm and 'tune'.

Once more unto the breach!

> *Once more unto the breach, dear friends, once more;*
> *Or close the wall up with our English dead.*
> *In peace there's nothing so becomes a man*
> *As modest stillness and humility:*
> *But when the blast of war blows in our ears,*
> *Then imitate the action of the tiger;*
> *Stiffen the sinews, summon up the blood,*
> *Disguise fair nature with hard-favoured rage;*
> *Then lend the eye a terrible aspect;*
> *Let it pry through the portage of the head*
> *Like the brass cannon; let the brow o'erwhelm it*
> *As fearfully as doth a galled rock*
> *O'erhang and jutty his confounded base,*
> *Swill'd with the wild and wasteful ocean.*
> *Now set the teeth and stretch the nostril wide,*
> *Hold hard the breath and bend up every spirit*
> *To his full height. On, on, you noble English.*

As you read you should be aware of these interesting points that are relevant to the exercise.

Some of the words are shortened with expected letters missing signalled by an apostrophe, such as 'O'erhang' instead of overhang. This has the effect of reducing the word by one syllable, thus balancing the rhythm of the metre within the line.

Some of the lines fit the rules of iambic pentameter perfectly and others break the rule to differing degrees.

Sometimes the meaning and sense of what is being said takes a natural pause at the end of a line but sometimes it flows through to the next. In some cases it takes a natural stop mid-line with a new sentence then starting. However, the rhythm, tune and sense of the speech are implicitly linked – working always together and never in competition with each other.

Now speak the speech out loud, purposely and artificially exaggerating the rhythm of the iambic pentameter in those lines where it is perfectly formed. As you do this, really get a feeling for the structure and shape of the rhythm (spoken in this accentuated way, it should have a very bouncy feel to it) and note where the rhythm departs from the usual metre and the effect this has on the overall tune.

Next, speak these specific lines which are all 'pure' iambic lines and are here split up into their metrical feet and with the beat stresses indicated in bold type – so, just for the time being, really 'hammer home' the rhythm, making it painfully obvious to any listener (imagined or otherwise) and forgetting all other concerns at this stage. You will notice that a metrical foot will sometimes cut through a single word.

*Once **more**/ un**to**/ the **breach**/, dear **friends**/, once **more**/;*
*But **when**/ the **blast**/ of **war**/ blows **in**/ our **ears**/,*
*Stiff**en**/ the **sin**/ews, **sum**/mon **up**/ the **blood**/,*
*Now **set**/ the **teeth**/ and **stretch**/ the **nost**/ril **wide**/,*

Now speak the following lines, which are not purely iambic and which break the rule. The iambic metre has been divided and notated in the same way but now with the extra offending syllable or beats indicated by being underlined – emphasize the discrepancy so that you begin to feel and echo the full complexity of the tune in your voice. You will see how the extra beats add dramatic emphasis to the words and colour to the tune. Again, exaggerate and do not worry about meaning and acting in this exercise – you are purely concerned here with hearing the tune powerfully clearly and embedding it in your mind and soul. Also of interest here is the way the word

'imitate' is not only split between two metrical feet, but the second of these feet has only one of the word letters – 'i' – in the first of its two beats.

*Then **im**/i**tate**/ the **ac**/tion **of**/ the **ti**/<u>ger</u>;*
*Like **the**/ brass **can**/non; **let**/ the **brow**/ o'er-**whelm**/ <u>it</u>*
*To **his**/ full **height**./ On, **on**/, you **no**/ble **Eng**/<u>lish.</u>*

Return now to the whole speech and speak it again aloud, this time reducing the amount of unnatural emphasis by approximately half. It should still sound false and 'over-the-top' but the normality of expression and elucidation should begin to return and exert themselves.

Repeat again, reducing the exaggeration now to around ten per cent of its original intensity.

Finally, for this exercise, return to speaking the lines normally, without the considerable emphasis you have been placing upon the rhythm, but still be actively aware of its presence and how it works tirelessly beneath the words. Replace the subtlety and acting that were withheld before, and let the words flow in a way which you think best illuminates and communicates the speech. You will find that the rhythmical musicality of the piece will automatically be retained implicitly and you will begin to realize how it refuses to be ignored rather than needing to be revealed.

THE MELODY OR THE TUNE

The almost vulgar simplicity of this last exercise should have really started a process of realization within you that Shakespearean verse-speaking is far easier and more organically present in, and obtainable from, the actual writing than you may first have imagined. You should certainly now feel more at ease with its speaking, and have begun to find that the only danger it really presents is when it is feared, avoided or ignored.

It is important, at this stage, to realize also that 'hearing the tune' of the verse refers to just that – the tune – and not only the rhythm. By now the rhythm should be obvious, not to say unavoidable, but you may find it harder to associate speaking the lines with some form of melody. However, while, for the most part, Shakespeare's plays are not written in song, the verse particularly requires a wide range of notes within the actor's voice, and the rising and falling of the cadences within the text give strong musical leads as to how the vocal instrument should be played.

Obviously, the tune associated within a Shakespearean speech or dialogue is not as rigidly interpretable as a song is, with its specific notes and intervals. It is a tune which is far more flexible and improvisational, but it is a tune nonetheless, and all of the information the actors requires for its 'playing' can be found amongst the verse.

EXERCISE – VERSE-SPEAKING (3)

Really Hearing the Tune

As before, begin by reading the following words quietly to yourself, in order to become familiar with their sound in your head. It is a speech of Rosaline's from Act V, scene ii, of *Love's Labours Lost*.

> They are worse fools to purchase mocking so.
> That same Biron I'll torture ere I go:
> O that I knew her were but in by the week!
> How I would make him fawn, and beg, and seek,
> And wait the season, and observe the times.

Handy Hint 14

Acting Masculine or Feminine

In those blank verse lines that have eleven syllables instead of the standard ten – in other words, they do not fit the pattern – the extra syllable may be evident at the beginning or the end of the line. Each of these alternatives affords you an opportunity to use them for specific 'acting' emphasis.

A masculine beginning – where the extra beat can be stressed at the beginning of the line, or where the first two beats of a ten-beat line will not fit the unstressed/stressed pattern because their natural emphasis reverses this or presents two stresses – affords you the chance to grab the audience's attention or focus the content of the coming line or lines. This beginning can often manifest itself as an exclamation such as 'Ha', 'O' or 'What'.

A feminine ending – the extra syllable being unstressed at the end of an eleven beat line – allows you to promote an unfinished or contemplative sound. It can be used to emphasize an emotion or to 'trail-off' a thought or word.

> And spend his prodigal wits in bootless rhymes,
> And shape his service wholly to my hests
> And make him proud to make me proud that jests!
> So perttaunt-like would I o'ersway his state,
> That he should be my fool, and I his fate.

Now speak it out loud, with a reasonable amount of volume, and, as before with the sonnet exercise, see how many variations of pitch you can apply to the words. Let your speaking voice move up and down its scale as you find the appropriate expression, colour and emphasis for the speech.

That he shall be my fool.

Having done this, you are now going to take the idea a step further. Repeat the speech but, this time, sing it rather than speak it; improvise a tune that flows from line to line and visits as many different notes as possible. Do not worry about the quality of your singing voice; simply concentrate on the extra freedom of pitch variation that singing the words can easily give to the lines. It is not at all necessary to create a recognizable song structure that repeats a tune or has verse and chorus sections – the tune may be allowed to move happily along, changing and developing as it goes. Don't forget the rhythm as you do this; let the tune speed up and slow at appropriate places while, at the same time, ensuring that it runs up and down as many notes within the key as possible.

Next, stop singing and return to speaking the words. Although you will not remember your improvised song, you should now be far more aware of the musicality of the speech, and the possibilities of 'song' within it. Your speaking voice should find a wide variation of notes more easily and you should feel more connected to the tune that lies behind the spoken words.

APPLYING BREATH CONTROL

It is now an appropriate moment in your study of verse-speaking to be reminded of the breath control work undertaken in the previous chapter and apply it again, now with the additional focus upon rhythm, metrical structure and tune.

By now you should be fast becoming able to hear the 'tune' in your head, have an implicit concept of the musicality of what you are saying and be able to reflect these imaginatively in your speaking voice – in other words you are finding and perfecting the basic foundations of verse-speaking. However, there is absolutely no point whatsoever in acquiring this understanding if your breathing technique then lacks the skill and ability to apply it effectively.

Therefore, it must be your next priority to combine these two important elements and discover how one supports the other. With your vocal work so far you should be developing the technique of rhythmical and melodic recognition, plus that of deep, full and (most importantly) controlled breathing – along with precision and dexterity of diction. Now is the time to marry all of these together into the whole that is Shakespearean verse-speaking.

Handy Hint 15

Avoiding the Fall

One of the most important faults to be avoided when speaking verse is a falling ending to the line. Iambic pentameter is a rising rhythm, due to the nature of its weak/strong pattern, and this intrinsic structure needs to be encouraged and not thwarted. In most instances, the rhythm must constantly move forward with each line rising into the next. If you let your voice drop in tone, volume or pitch too habitually as you reach metrical pauses, you will find that your verse-speaking becomes turgid.

Where possible, you should lift the end of the line in expectation of what is to follow and this will, as well as giving the verse momentum and drive, move the sense of what you are saying forwards dynamically and make you interesting to listen to.

Of course, it is your acting that is paramount in all of this and this will necessitate some not infrequent breaking of this rule. However, in general, you should keep the energy of your verse-speaking up and thrusting, even when you are involved in acting the more downbeat emotions.

EXERCISE – VERSE-SPEAKING (4)

Verse-Speaking Takes Shape

Begin by reading the following two speeches from *Romeo and Juliet* quietly in your head to establish a feeling for mood and content. They are speeches of Romeo from Act II, scene ii, and Juliet from Act III, scene ii, respectively and can both be used within the exercise or simply the one pertinent to your sex if you prefer. Most importantly, they both contain considerable musicality of verse and demanding breathing requirements at certain places within them.

Romeo: But soft, what light through yonder
 window breaks?
It is the east, and Juliet is the sun.
Arise. Fair sun, and kill the envious moon,
Who is already sick and pale with grief,
That thou her maid art far more fair than she:
Be not her maid, since she is envious;
Her vestal livery is but sick and green,
And none but fools do wear it; cast it off.
It is my lady; O, it is my love!
O, that she knew she were!
She speaks yet she says nothing: what of that?
Her eye discourses: I will answer it.
I am too bold, 'tis not to me she speaks:
Two of the fairest stars in all the heaven,

O Romeo, Romeo!

Having some business, do intreat her eyes
To twinkle in their spheres till they return.
What if her eyes were there, they in her head?
The brightness of her cheek would shame those
  stars,
As daylight doth a lamp; her eyes in heaven
Would through the airy region stream so bright
That birds would sing and think it were not
  night.
See, how she leans her cheek upon her hand!
O, that I were a glove upon that hand,
That I might touch that cheek!

Juliet: *Gallop apace, you fiery-footed steeds,*
Towards Phoebus' lodging: such a wagoner
As Phaethon would whip you to the west,
And bring in cloudy night immediately.
Spread thy close curtain, love-performing night,
That runaways' eyes may wink, and Romeo
Leap to these arms, untalk'd of and unseen.
Lovers can see to do their amorous rites
By their own beauties; or, if love be blind,
It best agrees with night. Come, civil night,
Thou sober-suite matron, all in black,
And learn me how to lose a winning match,
Play'd for a pair of stainless maidenhoods:
Hood my unmann'd blood bating in my cheeks
With thy black mantle, till strange love grown
  bold
Think true love acted simple modesty.
Come night; come, Romeo, come, thou day in
  night;
For thou wilt lie upon the wings of night
Whiter than new snow on a raven's back.
Come, gentle night, come, loving, black-brow'd
  night,
Give me my Romeo; and, when he shall die,
Take him and cut him out in little stars,

The 'balcony scene' is ideal for rehearsing in the open air.

And he will make the face of heaven so fine,
That all the world will be in love with night,
And pay no worship to the sun.

Now you should not only speak them out loud, but really perform them. Experiment with all that you have learned so far and enjoy all of your verse-speaking, breathing, articulation and interpretational skills. If you are slightly too mature to be playing these parts, fear not: throw caution to the wind and relive your youth with gusto.

6 MOVING SHAKESPEARE

Leo Wringer (Fool) in the RSC's production of King Lear *at the Albery Theatre in London, 2005. (Photo: Robbie Jack)*

YOU MUST MOVE TO BE MOVING

In view of the fact that Shakespeare's plays are full of the most beautiful words, arranged into wonderful patterns of poetic verse, and also in view of the fact that these words have such great meaning, significance and resonance that they have been debated, interpreted, and dissected constantly over several hundred years, it is little wonder that students of their performance may easily become so preoccupied with the vocal delivery that they completely forget that sound is but half the picture.

An actor has two principal instruments – voice and body. The latter of these is as vital to the success of their endeavours as the former. The incredible beauty of Shakespeare's words does not necessitate a lesser importance of movement than other forms of drama but, on the contrary, a greater one. Shakespeare, despite his genius as a poet, is first and foremost a playwright, and the very best of playwrights at that. Because of this, all of his exquisite words, however wonderful they are to listen to, are focused very strongly upon the illumination of character and situation. Movement is as important to character and situation as voice and, without an ability to move well and to possess a body that is flexible and expressive, any Shakespearean actor, however strong and effective their voice may be, is rendered totally unable to function effectively.

CENTRE

The first step in attaining good physicality is to lower your centre of gravity: to remove the unnecessary tension in the upper body and to

Physicality is all.

place more emphasis and focus upon the lower. A good way of thinking about this is to imagine that you are carrying the majority of your body weight below the waist instead of above it – this is called 'Weight Down' and the process of uniting upper and lower body in a holistically expressive whole is called 'Centring'.

The first step on the route to good centring is to find your 'Centre' and this is one of the most important things any actor can do. Your 'Centre' is the place within yourself where everything must emanate and then radiate – both feeling and expression. It is, if you like, your energy centre – a powerhouse of emo-

Handy Hint 16

Get Your Weight Down

One of the greatest barriers to expressive movement and physicality is when an actor has too much tension in the upper part of the body. Human beings are extremely intelligent and reasoning animals and our existence is, of course, dominated by our brains: we live in our heads and our whole concept of body and soul emanates from there. Because of this we tend to pull the emphasis of our expression and communication upwards as we gesture with our hands and arms, open and close across our chests, shrug and raise our shoulders, manipulate our facial features and speak through our mouths.

We tend to forget that our whole body is capable of expression and consider that, in terms of communicating; everything below chest level is simply there to carry the expressive devices above it around. However, our whole bodies are expressive and any characters that we play are defined in terms of a complete person and a whole and totally integrated body.

Of course, a great deal of communication does take place in the upper body but an overemphasized perception of this leads to too much muscular activity and stress and inhibits and blocks the very process of expression itself.

So you must make sure that you carry your weight, and the majority of your body's tension, below the waist. You must also aim to be more in contact with the ground and less with the sky. You must get your 'weight down'.

tional electricity from which all of your acting springs: it is the centre of your acting soul.

Our human perception of 'soul' is often linked to our hearts, where we sense both a metaphorical and physical connection to feeling. Although an actor's heart is obviously an important feature because of this, it is still perhaps too high in the body to be their 'Centre'. This can be envisaged still lower, right down in the stomach area – the gut. We often talk of having 'a gut feeling' and emotional pain is often metaphorically attributed to this area when we talk of receiving a shock, like a blow to the stomach for instance. We also talk of someone having 'guts', usually meaning that their personal courage and determination goes deep down within them.

It is somewhere down between your heart and your gut that you must find your own centre. Its exact location will differ from person to person, but it must be the area of your body from which you feel your emotional being has its source. Having found it you will then be able to use it as starting point for all of your acting, including your voice and physical expression.

EXERCISE – FINDING YOUR CENTRE (1)

Finding It Physically
Get any normal chair and sit with your bottom close to the edge of it, keeping your back straight to begin with.

Keep your legs straight and place the heels of your feet upon the floor, keeping them flexed with toes pointing upwards – your legs should be comfortably wide apart, creating a V or triangular shape in front of you.

Hold your arms out straight in front of you, parallel to the angle of your legs and with your hands just slightly lower than your shoulders.

Find your centre!

Keep your palms open and your fingers relaxed.

Now imagine that someone has gently pushed your stomach inwards. Do not harshly contract your stomach muscles but just let your tummy move inwards a little and, at the same time, let your arms and legs bend slightly at elbow and knee. Relax any rigidity in your back and lean forward slightly – keeping your head level and your eyes up and forwards.

You should now not only feel your whole body emanating from a central point but also that your upper and lower body, including arms, legs and head, forms an expressive opening that offers outwards, directing and channelling from this central point.

Finding It Emotionally

Read to yourself the following highly emotional speeches. There is a choice of two to work upon – the words of the eponymous hero from *Titus Andronicus*, Act III, scene i, if you are male, or those of Lady Anne from Act I, scene ii, of *Richard the Third*, if you are female.

Titus Andronicus:

It was my dear, and he that wounded her
Hath hurt me more than had he killed me dead;
For now I stand as one upon a rock,
Environed with a wilderness of sea,
Who marks the waxing tide from wave by wave,
Expecting ever when some envious surge
Will in his brinish bowels swallow him.
This way to death my wretched sons are gone;

Here stands my other son, a banished man,
And here my brother, weeping at my woes.
But that which gives my soul the greatest spurn
Is dear Lavinia, dearer than my soul.
Had I but seen thy picture in this plight,
It would have madded me; what shall I do
Now I behold thy lively body so?
Thou hast no hands to wipe away thy tears,
Nor tongue to tell me who hath martyred thee;
Thy husband he is dead, and for his death
Thy brothers are condemned, and dead by this.

Lady Anne:

Set down, set down your honourable load,
If honour may be shrouded in a hearse;
While I awhile obsequiously lament
Th' untimely fall of virtuous Lancaster.

Poor key-cold figure of a holy king!
Pale ashes of the house of Lancaster!
Thou bloodless remnant of that royal blood!
Be it lawful that I invocate thy ghost
To hear the lamentations of poor Anne,
Wife to thy Edward, to thy slaughtered son,
Stabb'd by the self-same hand that made these
   wounds.
Lo, in these windows that let forth thy life
I pour the helpless balm of my poor eyes.
Curs'd be the hand that made these fatal holes!
Cursed the heart that had the heart to do it!
Cursed the blood that let this blood from hence!
More direful hap betide that hated wretch
That makes us wretched by the death of thee
Than I can wish to adders, spiders, toads,
Or any creeping venom'd thing that lives!

The anguish of Titus.

If ever he have child, abortive be it,
Prodigious, and untimely brought to light,
Whose ugly and unnatural aspect
May fright the hopeful mother at the view,
And that be heir to his unhappiness!
If ever he hath wife, let her be made
More miserable by the death of him
Than I am made by my young lord and thee!

Acquaint yourself fully with the situation and meaning of the speech by reading the play, studying a plot synopsis, using a set of notes for the lines in question or, ideally, a combination of all three.

Next spend some time thinking about the emotional content of the speech. Consider what you think the character is feeling and the pain, anguish and anger that they are encountering. Try to put yourself in their position and find a personal reaction to the words they use – what does their emotion mean to you and how does it affect you?

Select six individual words from the speech that you consider to be the most emotionally resonant: words that encapsulate the power and energy of the speech for you. These six can be entirely your own choice and each individual actor's list may be very different according to their own emotional reaction to the speech. An example of a possible list from each of the male and female speeches is:

Titus – *dead, bowels, banished, woes, martyred, condemned*
Anne – *lament, lamentations, wounds, cursed, creeping, miserable*

Take each of the words in turn to work upon them individually.

Think about the word and concentrate

While I awhile obsequiously lament.

upon its emotional significance and power. Now visualize that word existing deep down within yourself. Imagine it to be an ache or pain right in the very middle of you. Do not think about the word's intellectual meaning but concentrate upon it as a feeling, like an emotional lump of energy within you. Feel a physical rather than a cerebral reaction to it as if the word were the emotion it invokes itself. It may help to envisage the word as a light burning brightly deep down within you

Try to locate where within your body you feel that this word now sits. If you feel that it is too high – too near to your head or even your heart – let it sink down further towards your gut. Where it comes to rest is the place from where your emotional acting energy must always originate and spring – it is your 'Centre'.

Now feel the word beginning to grow, to become too large to remain within you. Also feel that it burns brighter and brighter, becoming too hot and energized to remain located where it is. Take a long deep and relaxed breath right down to where the word is.

Expel the breath and let the word ride up and out of you, vocalizing it as it leaves your mouth. The word should not necessarily sound normal or meaningfully inflected – it should emerge as a very guttural, primeval utterance, full of your own perception of the emotional significance it has attained while inside you as an individual actor, unique from any other. It should sound like an emotionally charged noise and not necessarily recognizable as the word at all. A helpful, if rather unpleasant, image of this expulsion of sound might be that of vomiting it forth from deep within you.

Repeat this for each of the words in turn, taking plenty of time to establish their own individual power and emotional significance.

Next return to the first word in the list and repeat the process as before. However, this time allow an appropriate gesture, movement or both to accompany the sound. You must make sure that this movement, whatever it is and of whatever size, originates and radiates from exactly the same place as the sound. Not only must its emotional impetus begin here, in tandem with the word, but it must physically manifest itself from here also. For example: if you feel the impetus to raise both your hands in front of you in an open gesture of supplication – let your hands grow forwards and out

from the area of your centre, keep your shoulders down and feel that your arms open out from your centre in the same way as your legs. Repeat again for all the words.

Now leave the chair and position yourself in whatever way you feel that the character would be for the speech. Now speak through the whole speech, concentrating on finding the emotion deep down within your 'Centre' and feeling all physical communication – gesture, expression and body posture – emanating from there. If you find the character moving during the speech, make sure that every movement grows and leads from your 'Centre'.

ENERGY FROM THE EARTH

In your important quest to develop a general physicality that is well 'Centred' with your 'weight down' and without unnecessary tension located in the upper part of your body, it will be extremely helpful for you to visualize a source for the power and energy you use as an actor.

Shakespeare demands extraordinary levels of energy, both emotionally and physically. Not only does it take physical strength and endurance to sustain a long, leading Shakespearean role, but the characters are so powerfully charged and dynamic that portraying them at all requires great reserves of energy.

As has already been made clear, this energy must not translate into tension and it should dwell and radiate from the performer's 'Centre'. However, it will be beneficial for you to consider (metaphorically if you wish) where this energy comes from and how it enters your body.

In order to pull focus away from your head and upper body, visualize your source of energy flowing up from the earth below, through your feet and into the depository fuel tank of your 'Centre'. This image, while to an extent spiritual, is not without a very relevant physical context. The earth is, of course, all-important to the life of us human beings. We grow from it and it sustains and protects us. However, as a race, we spend a great deal of our time removing ourselves from it: we concrete over it, we live in buildings rising above it, we insulate ourselves from it with shoes and clothes and we increasingly exist in a intellectually and cerebrally driven world removed from the more elemental forces around us. This is not an invocation to return to nature, strip naked and return to living as cavemen in order to act properly, but it is a reminder that there lies below our feet a great organic mass of energy and sustenance.

As human beings we tend to pull away from this elemental energy source but as actors we must 'plug ourselves back into it' and let its power flow up and through us. Thinking in this way is certainly the very best means of getting your 'weight down', losing the energetic emphasis in the upper part of your body and bringing your lower half 'back into play'.

EXERCISE – FINDING YOUR CENTRE (2)

Rediscovering the Earth

This exercise will work best outdoors and away from manmade material, so choose a fine day and find a suitable quiet park, field or garden in which to work.

Lie down on your back in as flat and comfortable place as you can find. Wear comfortable clothing and be barefoot or wear soft shoes.

Try to get as much of your body in contact with the ground as possible. Do this by taking deep breaths in and then, as you exhale, relax your body and let it sink down towards and into the earth. For the moment keep your feet flexed and out of contact with the ground so that the whole length of your legs stretch out along the ground.

When you feel totally relaxed and as connected to the earth as much as possible, you will be ready to begin freeing your imagination. Visualize yourself lying upon a huge ball that is spinning through space (we tend to forget that this is exactly what we are doing every day of our lives). Feel the gravity pulling you gently down, securing you safely to this ball. Feel also energy coming up through this ball and into you: a warm sustaining energy – not one that creates tension but one that engenders a feeling of relaxed but dynamic power within you.

Allow this energy now to manifest itself in the sound of a hum. Let this hum be at as low a note as is comfortable without straining, let it be audible without being too loud and breathe as often as necessary to keep it steady and constant.

Feel this hum spreading all around your body and visualize it as a great powerful energy buzzing within you. Just gently keep it going and stay relaxed but mentally alert.

Slowly and carefully stand up, continuing the hum as you do so. As the various areas of your body leave contact with the earth, feel that the energy flow from it remains constant and simply intensifies in the remaining contacting parts in order to maintain the same overall level. As your feet finally make contact with the ground they will inherit all of the power and you should sense this flowing up through your legs – still filling your body with exactly the same amount of energy. Continue to visualize the hum as that energy and feel its dynamism within you. Spread your feet and toes to enable as much conductivity as possible and feel that the majority of your body, while now obviously physically divorced from the earth, is still irrevocably connected to it via your feet and the energy flow.

Now walk around, continuing to hum, and feel your feet plugging back into the power source every time they step down. Do not feel heavy or clumsy but rather that you rise out of the earth in a totally relaxed way and that your movement is full of graceful energy sustained from below. Concentrate the effort of your movement below your 'Centre' and allow the upper part of your body to feel free, easy and devoid of unnecessary tension.

Having established this fundamental link with your energy source, this next exercise will help you to utilize the imagery practically.

Elemental Forces

In preparation, read through these lines which are a combination of words spoken by the witches in Act IV, scene I, of Shakespeare's play *Macbeth*, unified into one composite being which can be female or male.

Thrice the brinded cat hath mew'd.
Thrice and once the hedge-pig whin'd.
Harpier cries:– 'Tis time, 'tis time.
Round about the cauldron go;
In the poison'd entrails throw.
Toad, that under cold stone
Days and nights has thirty-one
Swelter'd venom sleeping got,

Boil thou first i' the charmed pot.
Double, double toil and trouble;
Fire burn, and cauldron bubble.
Fillet of a fenny snake,
In the cauldron boil and bake;
Eye of newt and toe of frog,
Wool of bat and tongue of dog,
Adder's fork and blind-worm's sting,
Lizard's leg and owlet's wing,
For a charm of powerful trouble,
Like a hell-broth boil and bubble.
Double, double toil and trouble;
Fire burn and cauldron bubble.
Scale of dragon, tooth of wolf,
Witches' mummy, maw and gulf
Of the ravin'd salt-sea shark,
Root of hemlock digg'd i' the dark,
Liver of blaspheming Jew,
Gall of goat, and slips of yew
Silver'd in the moon's eclipse,
Nose of Turk and Tartar's lips,
Finger of birth-strangled babe
Ditch-deliver'd by a drab,
Make the gruel thick and slab:
Add thereto a tiger's chaudron,
For the ingredients of our cauldron.
Double, double toil and trouble;
Fire burn and cauldron bubble.
Cool it with a baboon's blood,
Then the charm is firm and good.

Try to learn the speech or, at least part of it, so that you can work freely without the book in your hands.

Lie upon the ground as in the previous exercise. Relax yourself with breathing as before and allow yourself to experience the same connection.

Begin by visualizing the words slowly one by one. Imagine that they form way down

Double, double toil and trouble!

below you, deep in the earth – moving upwards into your body (not just your head), and then passing on upwards, out of you, via your mouth. Do not try to project, particularly enunciate or prettify the words – let them be guttural, primeval, as low in pitch as is comfortable and, above all, earthy in their quality.

Now stand up and repeat the exercise – this time feeling the words rising up out of the ground, through your feet, traversing up your whole body and being released through your head. Retain the same feeling of organic earthiness in the sound – you should imagine that you are a conduit for the words, allowing them liberation from the earth below you.

Continue to speak the lines, returning to the beginning at each completion so that they continue in an incanting round. However, now start to increase the speed a little and colour the lines so that your work becomes more of a performance. Use the rhythm and rhyming structure to maintain primeval atmosphere and persist in the image of the words emanating from the ground and growing up through you.

Finally add movement and gesture but make sure that every physical impulse starts within your 'Centre' and radiates evenly from it: bend your legs just as much as you raise your arms, keep as low to the ground as possible (as if your 'Hag' has appeared from the earth and keeps low to it ready to return), remain well balanced with your centre of gravity low and secure and allow your head movement, eye focus and facial expression to follow parallel to an imaginary line drawn out from your 'Centre'.

RELAXATION

There can be no doubt that a successful Shakespearean performer must devote a considerable proportion of their overall work to their physicality. After all, as important as the word may be, it is the body and its ability to characterize, communicate and express that an audience encounters most strongly when an actor first enters upon the stage.

However, all of this work is in great jeopardy and all bodily communications in danger of negation if unnecessary tension in the body is overly present. Indeed, tension in the body will not only impede physicality but will also permeate into the voice as well, completely undermining the vocal process and destroying the tone and quality of an actor's voice. It is for these reasons that tension is one of the greatest and most formidable enemies a Shakespearean actor (or, indeed, any actor) can encounter and, because it can be an ongoing problem, you should have a strategy in place to deal with it.

This strategy should be two pronged: addressing the root of tension, the mind, and the depository of tension, the body. By controlling the causes and also the remaining manifestations of tension, you should not be unduly troubled by this potential spoiler.

Tension originates in the mind as worry and doubt: worries from one's personal life, which are completely unconnected to the performance process, and doubts about one's ability as an actor, which are very much connected to the performance process. Shakespeare is full of emotional and intellectual challenges, and difficulties that exist within your own life may well distract and defocus you from the job in hand, creating conflict within you and leading to physical tension.

It is, of course, also in the actor's mind, that doubts and fears about their ability to rise to, and master, the challenges of the work are born and fostered. Hopefully, this book is leading you towards an ease and confidence in your Shakespearean performing abilities, but it would be dishonest not to acknowledge that all actors, however competent, talented and technically skilled they may be, suffer from time to time from self-doubt and fears of inadequacy. Indeed, an actor needs this vulnerability and danger as, without it, they would become arrogant, emotionally shallow and artistically under-developed – an actor who feels totally confident and safe will instinctively veer towards mediocrity. However, the further tension that may result is not desirable at all.

It is essential then that you begin your battle against tension at its source. While the aforementioned psychological preoccupations will never be totally eradicated, they can be managed and their effects considerably negated. The effort involved in this part of your strategy regarding tension will be amply rewarded and may well benefit your life generally as well.

You must relax!

EXERCISE – CALMING THE MIND

Your Other Life

This exercise should be practised not only in relation to your studies now, but every time you begin to work either at home, in rehearsal or for a performance.

Sit comfortably in a quiet room, breathe slowly and deeply and allow your body and mind to let go of the stresses and strains of the day – and relax. Think about all the things that have nothing to do with your performance but are causing you concern or worry – these may be important problems, as well as simply things on your mind that need to be done imminently. Create a mental list of these.

In your imagination create a box – one that is not too large to be carried easily, were it real. Mentally open the box and, from your list, place each of its items, one by one, safely into the box. Then see yourself closing the box and locking it.

In your mind, write on the top of the box a time when you know that you will have finished your performance work for the day and when you will be able to reassess the items within it and deal with them again. Give yourself permission to open it then but not before.

Performing Confidence

This exercise should also be practised regularly and especially when you are about to work.

Try to relax fully, as in the previous exercise. Make sure that you are dressed not only comfortably, but in clothes which make you feel good and confident.

Pick your favourite piece of text – play, poem or prose, by Shakespeare or another author. Stand up and perform the piece aloud – using appropriate movement if required.

Enjoy the wonderful sound of your own unique voice. Listen to its tone, cadences and diction.

Move fluently, dynamically and confidently. Concentrate on every part of your body as it moves and feel good about yourself.

Now sit down and with pen and paper write a list of all the plus points about your acting – every element of your body, voice and mind that contributes to your success as a performer. Do not be modest (this list is for your eyes only) so get every possible attribute down upon the paper.

Now write a second, honest, list of those qualities that you feel need improvement – not to be thought of as 'bad' you will notice, but those requiring attention.

Lastly, next to these attention points write what you consider needs to be done in order to improve them or eradicate them all together.

You are now ready to begin work positively and with realistic confidence.

Both of these psychological exercises are designed to put you in a frame of mind that will produce useable, dynamic energy as you work, rather than destructive tension.

EXERCISE – CALMING THE BODY

The mind can also address the muscles of the body directly – in a positive way – in order to reduce unnecessary tension and promote relaxation. Remember though that, in terms of performing, some tension is required in the body for it to function (devoid of tension, for instance, you would simply fall over) and all of the unnecessary tension that you eradicate must be replaced with 'relaxed energy' – this should not be a relaxation regime to make you sleep.

Lie upon the floor (indoors for this one), with your legs flexed and your feet flat upon the floor, and your head supported to a comfortable height with a suitable pile of books. Begin, as usual, with some deep, relaxing breathing.

Starting with your toes and moving slowly along your body towards your head, tense each of your muscle groups in turn, hold the tension and then let them release and fully

Be honest about yourself.

relax. Don't forget the hands and arms as you work along.

As you do this, let each relaxation sink the muscles concerned down into the floor, leaving your body feeling relaxed and heavy.

Now concentrate particularly upon your breathing. Breathe in deeply through your nose and imagine that this inward breath is filling the whole of your body with energy – as if it were lighting it up with a bright light. Exhale through your mouth and imagine that this outward breath is expelling all of the tension from your body. You breathe 'in' energy and 'out' tension. Continue with this breathing pattern for at least five minutes.

Slowly and carefully stand up and gently shake out your limbs.

All three of the relaxation exercises you have undertaken should be useful to you, but you should seek out more (even invent your own if you wish): an ongoing focus upon relaxation is essential for all actors. Remember, you are the very stuff of your artistic expression – you use no paintbrush, musical instrument or potter's wheel, for example – and, therefore, you must work to be tension-free on stage as much as is possible. Like everything connected to dramatic art, this will not be achieved without some effort.

STRETCHING

Actors need to be as limber as possible. The main focus of your limbering work should be upon stretching. Your muscles do not have to be developed or 'pumped' but it is essential that you are as physically loose and strong as your age and physique will allow. Your best plan will be to visit a regular dance class, but a

---

Handy Hint 17

Attain Responsive Physicality

An actor's body is their 'instrument' (along with the voice) and, as such, must be well tuned and responsive to the demands placed upon it by the 'player' – the actor's mind, heart and soul. While all dramatic literature 'worth its salt' is demanding on the practitioner's physicality, the classics, and especially Shakespeare, place particular emphasis on bodily flexibility, control and responsiveness.

Shakespeare demands truth and with it truthful acting. Therefore, physical expression, communication and characterization must be organic and natural, not forced or laboured. Naturalness and truth come from spontaneous physical adaptation, postural realignment and muscular dynamics: in order to achieve this, the actor does not necessarily need to possess an athletic body (this would be inhibiting to character anyway), but they do need to possess a limbered and flexible one. The kind of development an actor's body needs leans more to the world of dance than to that of sport but it is a very important development nonetheless.

Like voice, physical skills cannot be learned overnight and require you to engage with a long term project of sustained improvement. This project should start here and now and you will ignore this requirement at your peril.

---

gentle aerobic and stretching routine will serve you as a starting point and also as a regular physical warm-up. You should adapt this to suit your own needs, age and physical abilities – and be careful to approach it at a comfortable level of intensity.

EXERCISE – PHYSICAL WARM-UP AND GENTLE STRETCH

Employ the use of a mat or find a soft carpet to work upon. Dress in loose comfortable clothing with jazz (or other soft shoes) or bare feet.

Begin in a standing position with your feet approximately the same distance apart as your shoulders – toes turned out slightly. Flex your knees just a little so that your legs are not locked, let your arms hang loosely by your side, feel open across your chest with your shoulders gently back and keep your head level – looking straight ahead. Make sure that the majority of tension in your body is located below the waist, where it is relatively harmless, rather than in your upper half where it can do a great deal of harm to your expressive areas.

Gently and slowly rotate shoulders and neck (for several rotations each and reversing direction occasionally) in order to ease out these two prime areas for harbouring tension. There is no need to drop your head completely back as you rotate (as this can be dangerous); neither should these actions be energetic or strenuous – just a gentle easing and stretching.

Shake your arms and hands as well as your legs and feet (alternately, of course) and move them about in the air around you as you do this. Again, do this very gently and try to retain reasonable balance. There is no need to be frantic at all with this – you are simply getting the blood flowing.

Bend your knees and swing your arms in a skiing motion. Continue this, letting your knees bend just a little more each time and your arms float a little higher – until they are swinging up parallel with the ground in front of you – automatically with the momentum,

without great effort and keeping your shoulders from rising up towards your ears. Continue for around thirty repetitions and this will aerobically warm you still further.

Operating from your 'Centre' as always, stretch and lunge (with arms and legs) around and out into the area around you. This should be kept slow and acutely controlled – almost as if in slow motion. Keep pulling this movement back in to yourself, and then push out in different directions. In your mind draw an imaginary, three dimensional, bubble all around a centre point where you are standing and then explore this space in every direction – up, sides, behind and downwards. Keep working from your 'Centre', keep controlled, don't raise your shoulders unnecessarily high and don't force any of the actions – just explore the space with smooth-flowing, easy movement. Continue this for approximately two minutes and then return to your still starting position – checking your posture as before.

Let your head drop onto your chest, then let your shoulders fall forward. Bending from the waist (and keeping your knees flexed), continue the movement forwards and downwards until you are hanging down like a rag doll. Make sure that your neck is relaxed and your head hangs freely – your hands should brush the floor. Gently bounce a few times. Slowly straighten up to standing again – making sure the head comes up last.

Lie down on your back, with your feet flexed (heels on the floor) and your arms by your side with palms uppermost. This is your basic position ready for the next few parts of the routine.

Lift your right leg slowly up (keeping the knee straight and now pointing the foot), until it is as near to a right angle to your torso as you

Fully explore the space.

can comfortably manage and your toe points upwards.

Now slowly flex your foot – you will feel a gentle stretch in your calf muscles as you do this. Point it again (slowly, do not rush) and then continue to flex and point for around twenty repetitions.

Next slowly lower your leg back down to the floor. You will feel the gentlest of 'pulls' in your stomach muscles as you do this. Repeat the whole process with your left leg.

Returning to your right leg – lift the knee up towards your head and place your hands around your leg under the knee. Pull your knee towards your chest, hold it for one second

and then release. Repeat this for ten repetitions. Again, repeat this process with the left leg.

Now pull your feet up towards your bottom and place your soles together – forming a rough triangular type shape between your legs. Gently bounce your knees down towards the floor for around twenty repetitions, but do not expect much movement here unless you are already very supple, but you should feel a little stretching.

Return your feet back to resume the basic lying position. Next pull both of your knees up towards your chest and then, keeping your feet flexed this time, straighten your legs as much

Stretch those legs!

as you can so your soles are uppermost. As with all these movements, do not push your body too far beyond its comfort zone – just let it do a little more work and stretching than usual.

Now open your legs as wide as they will go without strain and bounce and stretch a little further for just five repetitions. You will feel a slight 'burn' here in your legs and in your stomach muscles. Do not overdo it though!

Bring your feet back together and then to the floor in an exact reversal of their assent.

If you feel able, repeat this whole last process once or twice but be careful not to over exert yourself. Slowly stand up, shake out gently and take some deep breaths.

Actors come in many different shapes and sizes. This is, of course, just as well, as the characters that they play come in many different shapes and sizes too. However, there is one common factor of physicality that should unite all actors and is particularly relevant for Shakespeare, and that is the ability to move well.

A definition of 'moving well' can be found in the context of what is required. What is required is a reasonable neutrality of movement from which physical characteristics of various characters may grow. If an actor moves heavily, with shoulders hunched, they may well be ideally suited to play an older more sedentary character, but they will find a younger more vibrant role a considerable stretch. In Shakespeare there are so many various and wonderful characterizations on offer within most age ranges, and these characterizations are often so potentially physically colourful that an actor seriously requires a body and physicality that will respond in a multitude of ways, working from a solid neutrality.

Therefore, every Shakespearean actor must seek this 'neutrality of moving well'. This does not mean that they need to become athletes or models or that their movement should be devoid of their own personality. However, it does mean that, within the limitations of their particular body shape, they need to be able to move with reasonable ease, grace, co-ordination, fluidity, centring (as already explored), balance, poise and, when required, speed.

The Importance of Sport

Modern life tends to make us lazy and physical

exercise is far more easily avoided than was the case for previous generations. We all need to move more, just get our bodies working and pushing them further than they are often used to. One of the very best things that you can do, in tandem with your particular performance studies, is to play some kind of sport regularly. It does not really matter which sport you choose as most will promote all of the physical aspects that are important to you in some degree. However, it is best to avoid sports that might overly develop particular muscle groups, particularly in the upper body. Obviously you will choose a sport that suits your age and physical abilities and you should be aware that the sport you choose does not have to be necessarily particularly frantic: even a gentle sport like bowls promotes excellent movement for, as the player bends and steps forward to deliver the bowl along a path traced by their eye line they are engaging in wonderful 'weight down' centring.

The important thing is to get out there and play, at whatever intensity and frequency you choose. There is nothing better for encouraging co-ordination and instinctively effective, economic and fluid movement.

EXERCISE – SPORTING SHAKESPEARE

Find an old tennis racket and a ball and repair to an outside wall that is suitable to hit the ball onto.

Play the solo game of hitting the ball against the wall repeatedly, letting it bounce on the ground first each time and keeping the sequence going for as long as possible before recovering the ball and starting again.

Be aware of the backswing and follow

through that you employ in each shot and how your legs bend and you step into the shot each time. Feel how these movements automatically come from your 'Centre'. Be aware too of your hand-to-eye co-ordination, how you remained balanced, how your body moves with instinctive obedience to the commands of your brain – these are all fine physical attributes for the actor.

In order to examine and explore how moving in this way can be applied to your work on Shakespearean performance, this children's game now changes a little and becomes a proper exercise. Learn one of the following pieces of text (male or female) so that you can speak it easily 'by heart' and without any reference to the book.

Research the meaning and content of the scene as ever. The first piece is Cassius' speech from Act I, scene ii, of *Julius Caesar*:

Why, man, he doth bestride the narrow world
Like a Colossus, and we petty men
Walk under his huge legs and peep about
To find ourselves dishonourable graves.
Men at sometime were masters of their fates.
The fault, dear Brutus, is not in our stars,
But in ourselves, that we are underlings.

The following words are spoken by Luciana in Act III, scene ii, of *The Comedy of Errors*:

And may it be that you have quite forgot
A husband's office? Shall, Antipholus,
Even in the spring of love, thy love springs rot?
Shall love, in building, grow so ruinous?
If you did wed my sister for her wealth,
Then for her wealth's sake use her with more
kindness,

Now start playing the 'ball against the wall' again and, when you have established a good rhythm, start to speak the lines of the speech. Continue speaking and playing – restarting the ball and the lines as each requires.

At first you will probably find that it is difficult to do both, your concentration being split, but persevere; as you get used to it, you should find that the speech begins to find a verbal punctuation, emphasis and shape through the movement. Continuing speaking even when you have to retrieve the ball – think of this as a game you just happen to be playing with the person you are talking to. Thus, the lines and movement should fuse together into an organically created scene; what is more, you will find that your movements will remain fluid, co-ordinated and appropriate to the intentions of that scene.

The speeches used here are ideal for the purpose in as much as both characters are saying something important that they are keen to communicate but with no great urgency or particular passion at the time. The exercise can be explored further, however, by using one of the following speeches from *Much Ado About Nothing* that display considerable anger and frustration. As before, learn one of the following pieces of text (one is spoken by a female, and the other by a male) so that you can speak it easily 'by heart' and without any reference to the book. This time they are both prose

Movement and coordination.

pieces. Don't forget to do a little research upon it – this cannot but help.

Firstly, some words spoken by Beatrice in Act II, scene i:

Why, he is the prince's jester, a very dull fool; only his gift is in devising impossible slanders; none but libertines delight in him, and the commendation is not in his wit but in his villainy, for he both pleases men and angers them, and then they laugh at him and beat him. I am sure he is in the fleet; I would that he had boarded me.

The next speech is by Benedick in Act II, scene i:

O, she misused me past the endurance of a block! An oak but with one green leaf on it would have answered her; my very visor began to assume life and scold with her. She told me, not thinking that I was myself, that I was the prince's jester, that I was duller than a great thaw; huddling jest upon jest with such impossible conveyance upon me that I stood like a man at a mark, with a whole army shooting at me.

Now start playing the ball against the wall yet again and, just as before, when you are ready, start to speak the lines. Continue speaking and playing – restarting the ball and the lines as each requires.

This time the anger and vehemence in the speech (quite explosive for Benedick, quite calculated for Beatrice) should punctuate the movement more dynamically and you will find yourself playing the game more aggressively with a different pace and fluency of movement. Monitor how the words affect the movement and the movement affects the words.

You can try these exercises kicking a football or engaging in another suitable sporting activity if you wish.

An Important Lesson Learned

It is interesting to note here that, as the acting part of the exercise develops dramatically and with more intensity, so the movement changes. However, the most important factor to note is how the movement, instinctive and co-ordinated by virtue of the ball game, feeds back into the acting – indeed, becomes the acting itself. This is achieved because you are moving 'well'. The very nature of the game here instigates good movement almost without your being aware of it. Your aim should be to move closer and closer to this ease of movement and, having seen what it can achieve, you should be encouraged to pursue a sporting hobby as well as continuing with the exercises in this chapter.

MOVING, INTENTIONS AND THE PROBLEM OF INHIBITION

One of the fundamental causes which drives movement on stage is 'intention' – the reason for the move linked to what the character is doing at the time. This in itself can be a useful factor to explore as, by focusing upon it, an organic ease of movement can be discovered.

Concentrating upon reasons and intentions for moving is also an effective weapon in the battle against self-conscious and inhibited movement on stage. In life we are rarely self-conscious about our movement, simply because movement is a means to an end, a device for enabling us to pursue our tasks and requirements in our daily lives. On stage, because we are conscious of ourselves as performers, we can be tempted to think too much about movement, losing its spontaneity in exchange for awkwardness: one can often hear a struggling actor exclaim that they do not know what to do with their hands, for instance – something that tends not to be a concern at all in life.

This problem of inhibition can be bad enough in a modern play, where at least the imaginary environment inhabited is of some direct relevance. However, it becomes further magnified because of an actor's habitual (although unfounded) belief that Shakespeare is removed from their experience and rarefied in its execution.

As with so much of acting, solving the problem is very much a matter of acquiring a technique that allows the actor to 'tap into' the naturalness and normality of their everyday lives, and the key technique triggered here is almost certainly 'intention'.

EXERCISE – SMOOTHING MOVEMENT THROUGH INTENTION

For this exercise you will need to work with a fellow actor of the opposite sex or imagine the participation of a partner in the scene.

Look carefully at the following scene, a dialogue between Silvius and Phebe in Act III, scene v, of *As You Like It*, in preparation to work on one of the parts according to your gender. It will be very helpful for you to learn the words but not essential to the exercise.

> *Silvius:* Sweet Phebe, do not scorn me; do not, Phebe.
> Say that you love me not; but say not so in bitterness.

The common executioner, whose heart the accustomed sight of death makes hard,
Falls not the axe upon the humbled neck but first begs pardon.
Will you sterner be than he that lives by bloody drops?

Phebe: *I would not be thy executioner;*
I fly thee, for I would not injure thee.
Thou tell'st me there is murder in mine eye.
'Tis pretty sure, and very probable,
That eyes that are the frailest and softest things,
Should be called tyrants, butchers, murderers!
Now I do frown on thee with all my heart,
And if my eyes can wound, now let them kill thee.
O, for shame, for shame,
Lie not to say my eyes are murders.

Silvius: *O dear Phebe,*
If ever you meet in some fresh cheek the power of fancy,
Then shall you know the wounds invisible
That love's keen arrows make.

Phebe: *But till that time, come thou not near me*
And when that time comes, afflict me with thy mocks, pity me not;
As till that time, I shall not pity thee.

Because reason and intention are so important to this exercise, you should now study the following modern translation into a simpler rendition of the words (matched line for line) in order to be sure, before you start properly, what is happening and what you are saying. This will save you the usual research, although you may still refer to a published text with notes for extra enlightenment if you wish. However, it should be noted that the original scene has been edited for purpose and will not correspond exactly with other versions. This version endeavours to capture the spirit of the original and not an exact alternative for the words.

Silvius: Dear Phebe, please don't be horrible to
  me, Phebe – don't, Phebe.
You can say that you don't love me but don't say it
  so nastily.
Even an ordinary executioner, who is hardened by
  seeing death every day,
Doesn't kill anyone without saying sorry first.
Will you be crueller than someone who kills people
  for a living?

Phebe: I don't want to be your executioner.
I'm don't want you but I don't want to hurt you.
You say I have murder in my eyes.
It's very likely (I don't think!)
That eyes – the softest, most delicate parts of the
  body,
Should be able to butcher and kill tyrannically.
I'll try and stare at you as horribly as possible –
And if my eyes can wound, let's see if you drop
  down dead.
No, I thought not – shame on you!
Don't lie about my eyes being murderers!

Silvius: Oh, dearest Phebe –
If you ever meet somebody new and fall hopelessly
  in love,
Then you will know what invisible agony
Great Love can bring.

Phebe: Maybe, but until that happens keep away
  from me
But if it does happen, feel free to make fun of me
  and don't feel sorry for me.
Because, until it happens I'm not going to feel
  sorry for you.

Start by reading the scene and the alternative aloud with your partner (or read both parts if you are by yourself), and get a real feel for the thoughts behind the exchange. Work on both several times, really playing around and experimenting with the dialogue until it feels natural, spontaneous and comfortable. However, work only with the dialogue at this stage – do not move or block (devise moves and positions) it.

Now abandon the translation and work only with the proper scene.

Stand up with your partner (or alone if appropriate), agree a playing direction – that is where the audience would be if there were one, and make ready to move the scene by starting a reasonable distance apart and facing one another.

Using the following copy of the scene (which now contains instructions for movement in brackets) as your guide, begin the scene and move according to the directions.

Silvius: Sweet Phebe, [I want to be near her –
I love her so much – step towards her] *do not
scorn me; do not, Phebe.*
*Say that you love me not; but say not so in
bitterness.*
[I must make her understand how I feel – I
can't stand the pain of her hurting me – go
right up to her] *The common executioner, whose
heart the accustomed sight of death makes hard,*
*Falls not the axe upon the humbled neck but first
begs pardon.*
*Will you sterner be than he that lives by bloody
drops?*
[I want her to be sorry and comfort me – I'd
love it if she melted into my arms with remorse
– take several steps away and turn back on
her]

Phebe: [I'm not going to let him get away with that – he's so stupid I don't believe it – step towards him and lean head forwards] *I would not be thy executioner;*
I fly thee, for I would not injure thee.
[I need to move to release my tension – he talks such nonsense – walk further away from him as speaking] *Thou tell'st me there is murder in mine eye.*
'Tis pretty sure, and very probable,
That eyes that are the frailest and softest things,
Should be called tyrants, butchers, murderers!
[I want him to realize how stupid he is – he's really getting on my nerves, I could hit him – rush to him and swing him round] *Now I do frown on thee with all my heart,*
And if my eyes can wound, now let them kill thee.
[I want to accentuate my superiority – he's so easy to dominate – walk away from him, shaking head] *O, for shame, for shame,*
Lie not to say my eyes are murders.

Silvius: O dear Phebe,
[I've just thought of a good tactic and I must make the point – she'll fall for me when she hears this – go to her quickly] *If ever you meet in some fresh cheek the power of fancy,*
Then shall you know the wounds invisible
That love's keen arrows make.

Phebe: [I must shut him up and have the last word – he's so pathetic I hate him – push him across the stage with every line] *But till that time, come thou not near me*
And when that time comes, afflict me with thy mocks, pity me not;
As till that time, I shall not pity thee.

As you work through this, be aware that the bracketed instructions contain three elements

Sweet Phebe, do not scorn me!

divided by dashes. The first is the intention or motivation that instigates the move; then comes the feeling associated with the intention or motivation and thus powering the move; and finally the move itself.

As you work, do not dwell on the physical process of moving or worry about 'acting' the moves or 'characterizing' them – simply concentrate upon the intentions, motivations and feeling, and let the movement happen organically as a result of them. You should find that your movement becomes free-flowing and uninhibited.

Repeat the scene this way several times to really let it 'flow' physically.

Now change the movement in the scene – this time finding your own motivations, intentions and emotions to instigate and power them. However, make sure that you work these out in advance.

Finally, play the scene one last time – now having no preconceived plan for movement and just let it happen as it will. By now you should be moving so freely and purposefully that this added improvisational element will allow your physicality incredible expression and relevance. You will also now find that all of your moves are firmly rooted in motivation and thus completely truthful, natural and spontaneous.

THINKING, LOOKING AND MOVING

Although the last exercise is an immensely important one in terms of attaining a responsive and co-ordinated physicality for the Shakespearean actor, it does, paradoxically, highlight another problem. Because in most instances an actor knows when and how they are going to move on stage, they can forget the actual physical and mental mechanics of moving. In life we usually look to where we intend to move, check that it is safe for us to be there and that the move will facilitate the purpose that requires the move, and then we move. All of this is, of course, mainly subconscious but the process occurs nonetheless.

One of the factors that can lead to unnatural movement in theatre is that, because an actor moves because they have been 'blocked' to do so by the director or because they have decided upon that move in rehearsal, the move looks false in terms of its spontaneity. Although knowing the reasons for the move

greatly helps in this (in fact, it is essential), there can still be a problem if the actual process of meaning is not natural.

Therefore, when you are rehearsing a Shakespearean scene, you must remember not only to focus upon the motivation behind your movement but also the mechanics that afford the movement. It can be helpful to visualize the process and 'think – look – move'. You have already worked upon the thinking bit: now it is time to add the more physical elements.

EXERCISE – THINK, LOOK, MOVE

Familiarize yourself with one of the following speeches (male or female appropriately). There is no alternative version for these, so don't forget to check your understanding of them with a set of notes. Remember – you cannot act something you don't understand.

The first speech is spoken by a male, Antony, in Act III, scene ii, of *Julius Caesar*:

Friends, Romans, countrymen, lend me your ears;
I come to bury Caesar, not to praise him. [Move]
The evil that men do lives after them;
The good is oft interred with their bones;
So let it be with Caesar. [Move] The noble Brutus
Hath told you Caesar was ambitious:
If it were so, it was a grievous fault,
And grievously hath Caesar answer'd it.
Here, under leave of Brutus and the rest—
For Brutus is an honourable man;
So are they all, all honourable men—
Come I to speak in Caesar's funeral.
[Move] He was my friend, faithful and just to me:
But Brutus says he was ambitious;
And Brutus is an honourable man.
He hath brought many captives home to Rome

Whose ransoms did the general coffers fill:
[Move] *Did this in Caesar seem ambitious?*
When that the poor have cried, Caesar hath wept:
Ambition should be made of sterner stuff:
Yet Brutus says he was ambitious;
And Brutus is an honourable man.
[Move] *You all did see that on the Lupercal*
I thrice presented him a kingly crown,
Which he did thrice refuse: was this ambition?
Yet Brutus says he was ambitious;
And, sure, he is an honourable man.
[Move] *I speak not to disprove what Brutus*
  spoke,
But here I am to speak what I do know.
You all did love him once, not without cause:
What cause withholds you then, to mourn for
  him?
[Move] *O judgment! thou art fled to brutish*
  beasts,
And men have lost their reason. [Move] *Bear*
  with me;
My heart is in the coffin there with Caesar,
And I must pause till it come back to me.

The female speech is by Portia in Act IV, scene i, of *The Merchant of Venice*:

The quality of mercy is not strain'd,
It droppeth as the gentle rain from heaven
Upon the place beneath: [Move] *it is twice blest;*
It blesseth him that gives and him that takes:
[Move] *'Tis mightiest in the mightiest: it*
  becomes
The throned monarch better than his crown;
His sceptre shows the force of temporal power,
The attribute to awe and majesty,
Wherein doth sit the dread and fear of kings;
[Move] *But mercy is above this sceptred sway;*
It is enthroned in the hearts of kings,
It is an attribute to God himself;

And earthly power doth then show likest God's
When mercy seasons justice. [Move] *Therefore,*
  Jew,
Though justice be thy plea, consider this,
That, in the course of justice, none of us
Should see salvation: we do pray for mercy;
And that same prayer doth teach us all to render
The deeds of mercy. [Move] *I have spoke thus*
  much
To mitigate the justice of thy plea;
[Move] *Which if thou follow, this strict court of*
  Venice
Must needs give sentence 'gainst the merchant
  there.

Before you start, be aware that these pieces have been chosen for their persuasive qualities – both Antony and Portia are putting forward an argument, a strongly held view. For the purposes of this exercise, the circumstances of the scenes in the plays is not important. Antony is talking to many people but he is in front of them all, probably in an elevated position; Portia is talking directly to one person – Shylock. However, for the exercise, you should imagine that both characters are talking to many people and that they are in the middle of this group, surrounded by them in a large space.

It will be of enormous advantage (though not absolutely essential) for you to learn the words prior to attempting the exercise.

Find as large a room as possible in which to work. Imagine that this room is full of people, but each of these people just happens to look exactly like an object or piece of furniture within the room. For this reason you need to choose a room that has a fair amount of clutter.

Stand right in the middle of the room facing in any direction as a starting point.

Think, look, move.

Each speech has been punctuated with bracketed 'move' instructions. The rules of this exercise state that you must move at these points, and that the move must be a reasonably long one. Begin by addressing the text up to the first move point to the whole assembled crowd. This will necessitate turning as you speak and visually connecting with all of the various 'furniture' and 'object' people in the room – for the sake of convenience, we will call them 'Citizens' for both speeches.

At the first move point, decide that you wish to direct the next sentiment directly to one particular Citizen (*think*), turn around to make eye contact with one of them (*look*) – make sure that you lead this turn with the head and eyes, letting the body follow (this will promote

smooth and co-ordinated movement), and then go right up to that Citizen (*move*) in order to address the next words to them.

You can begin talking as you move or wait until you are in position, depending on how much importance you wish to give the words – pausing until you reach the Citizen will add weight and power to the sentiment, talking as you go will create pace and momentum. The important thing is to maintain eye contact with the chosen Citizen as you move towards them and then as you address them in position. You may feel a little strange talking to a chair or coat stand to begin with but you will get used to it.

At the next move point, decide that you now wish to speak directly with another Citizen somewhere else in the space. Repeat the process as before, remembering to think, look and move.

Continue in this way at every move point throughout the speech – except for the last, when you should return to centre and address the whole crowd of Citizens, turning around to all of them as before. Even here, though, try to lead the turn with your eyes and head.

You should find that this exercise really promotes a fluidity and purposeful nature to your movement but, above all, it should make it dynamic.

7 SHAKESPEAREAN CHARACTERIZATION

Simon Callow (Falstaff) and Judi Dench (Mistress Quickly) in the RSC's production of Merry Wives – The Musical *at Stratford-upon-Avon. (Photo: Robbie Jack)*

A Veritable Feast

When people think of performing Shakespeare with fear (as, hopefully, by now you do not), their first thoughts are always of the language, the difficulties and obstacles that they perceive to lurk within it. When most people think of performing Shakespeare with excitement and anticipation, their first thoughts are always of the wonderful array of characters on offer and the incredible fulfilling opportunities of dramatic endeavour that they afford them as actors.

The characters that so liberally people Shakespeare's plays are a rich and varied collection of colourful creations, created on the page with such detail, complexity and depth as to be quite breathtaking. There is simply no other playwright who can come close to matching Shakespeare's ability to give literary birth to such a large and exciting array of wonderfully constructed personifications of so many human characteristics, strengths, weaknesses and foibles. Indeed, all of human life and experience is here and the characters that can be encountered in Shakespeare cover, between them, an immense range of human traits and experience.

One of the acid tests of the sheer breadth of Shakespearean characterization is the fact that encountering his work will always instantly remind us of friends, colleagues, politicians, celebrities, people in the media, important figures in contemporary life, national heroes, infamous criminals, tragic icons and ourselves. In fact, all of human life is here!

When an actor approaches a Shakespearean characterization they should do so as a diner approaches a banquet – with their mouths

The joy of characterization.

watering in anticipation of the delicious, tangy, exotic but delicately balanced flavours that await them, cooked by a master chef. Shakespeare's feast, however, is not one confined to any one particular cuisine but a glorious 'spread' of every conceivable type of food from around the world, cooked in an endless variety of ways.

Characterization in General

Before looking at Shakespearean characterization itself, and the particular challenges it presents, it is essential to examine the fundamental truths that are associated with characterization generally. There are a certain number of important factors and rules that govern an actor's character-building and it will help immensely to examine and explore a summary of these.

* A playwright supplies certain information about their characters within the text of the play. This is perhaps by way of stage direction, as they make their initial entrance into the story, or by virtue of a written introduction in the front of the book, but is principally communicated within the words and actions of each character as he or she develops through the play. It is the actor's job to identify this information and, perhaps more importantly, interpret it – to 'dig out' the author's ideas about, and intentions for, the character. The amount, quality and depth of this information will vary, depending mostly upon the skill of the playwright; lesser-gifted writers often provide more stereotypical, caricatured cliché than they do hard facts and natural characteristics.

* An actor must use their imaginations to develop and expand detail about the character that they are playing. However good a playwright may be, there is always more that can be learned and deduced about a character, and part of an actor's skill is to fill in the gaps left by the author and devise certain facts and truths about the people that they are portraying, so as to breathe life into a three-dimensional creation. This, in a way, involves the actor becoming proactive in the creative fictional process, but they should be careful that any inventions of detail are true to, and in

keeping with, the author's original concept and intentions and do not take the character off in a direction that is not faithful to the play. Again, the amount, quality and difficulty of work needed here is very much dependent upon the playwright's abilities.

* However vivid and detailed a picture an actor has of a character – developed from the previous two points – it is vital to remember that all characterization has to be found within themselves. In an ideal world one could enter a dressing room at the 'half hour call' (thirty-five minutes prior to the commencement of the performance), take off oneself like a coat, hang it on a peg and take down a brand new person to wear for the play. Unfortunately this is not possible, as an actor's tool is themselves, and only themselves, and every actor is limited in their creative process by the body and soul that is uniquely and irrevocably theirs. Thus, all characterization is about finding the character within and not without: it is about a rearranging of self and a refocusing of priorities. You should not see this as a limiting factor but rather as an assurance that, however colourful a character may be, they will be assured of possessing naturalness and truth because they spring from the verifiably truthful and natural source that is you.

* A good play will always take its characters on a journey – something will happen to them as a result of the drama and they will never be quite the same people at the end as they were at the beginning. An actor must be aware of this journey and must take it also: they must have a clear concept of the

development of their role as the story progresses and they must know their character intimately at every stop along the way. Obviously, the longest and most obvious journeys are taken by the leading characters in a play but, if playing a smaller part, you must still find a progression for that character in some way – even one scene should affect any character involved in it to some degree. If it is not there, invent it: if all you have to do is come in and deliver a parcel in a scene for instance, admire a piece of furniture (or even a person) on the way out – thus, something has happened to you and, therefore, you must be real (not a very long or memorable journey perhaps, but a journey nonetheless).

✳ An actor must believe in the person they are playing if they are to expect an audience to believe in them. Therefore, however tempting it may be to 'go off at a tangent' and invent wild, romantic and exotic characteristics, always remember your watchword – 'truth'. At all costs keep characterization believable within the framework of the play. Look for the degree of reality that the playwright has set for the play and keep within its bounds.

✳ It is absolutely vital that all characterization is complete and full and inhabits every part of an actor's body, voice, head and heart. This does not mean to say that you have to actually become the character – playing them at the bus stop in some 'method-like' indulgence, for instance – but the moment you step upon the stage they must flow through, and exist in, all of you. This will not require you to forget yourself because 'yourself' is also needed on the stage – it is you and not the character that controls the pace, remembers the lines and the moves, monitors the audience's reactions, stops from falling off the edge of the stage and other technical niceties – but the characterization must be a unified whole.

SHAKESPEARE'S GIFT

Shakespeare's gift to you as an actor is the very finest raw material with which to work upon the former points as you could ever possibly wish for. Certainly, in terms of the first point – the information provided about the character – there is an absolute abundance on offer. All but the very smallest of Shakespearean roles come complete with whole panoply of facts about both the material and emotional lives of these fictional personages and even the smallest contain more helpful pointers than most playwrights could hope to provide.

If perhaps this truth is not always appreciated by every actor approaching Shakespeare, it is surely because of the perceived, but unfounded, difficulties that the text seems to present to them – difficulties that, by now, should be fast fading for you, if not disappeared altogether.

The way this information is provided by Shakespeare is twofold. The character's words and deeds tell much, of course, – with much layering of dramatic circumstances and personal motivation, ambition and intention (both honourable and otherwise). However, much is also depicted by means of other characters vocalized opinions of, and reactions to, their fellow inhabitant of the play. Indeed, such is the general depth and quality of Shakespeare's writing that character definition and delineation seem to ooze from the very pages of the plays themselves.

105

To prove this point to yourself (or to reinforce it if it does not need proving), the following exercise should be both interesting and enlightening.

EXERCISE – FINDING THE CHARACTER ON THE PAGE (1)

Select any key Shakespearean character, of either sex, from one of the plays with which you are reasonably familiar. Arm yourself with pen, paper and a comfortable chair.

Divide the paper into three columns, heading one 'Physical Characteristics', the second 'Personality Characteristics' and leave the third blank for use in the follow-up to this exercise.

Read through the entire play (not just the scenes the particular character is in) and write down every detail you can identify directly or deduce from every aspect of the text. You should find by the time you reach the last page of the final Act you will have a considerable list, which may even have developed onto further pieces of paper.

If, by any chance, this has not worked for you and you have found difficulty in extracting relevant information about your chosen person, the following more precisely focused exercise may be of assistance.

EXERCISE – FINDING THE CHARACTER ON THE PAGE (2)

Part 1
If you are not familiar with the play *Henry the Fifth*, read it through and/or watch one of the excellent film versions available. Familiarize yourself with the following speech from Act I,

scene ii, made by Henry to a messenger sent by the Dauphin of France. It is divided into numbered sections.

1. We are glad the Dauphin is so pleasant with us;
   His present and your pains we thank you for:

2. When we have march'd our rackets to these balls,
   We will, in France, by God's grace, play a set
   Shall strike his father's crown into the hazard.
   Tell him he hath made a match with such a wrangler
   That all the courts of France will be disturb'd
   With chases.

3. And we understand him well,
   How he comes o'er us with our wilder days,
   Not measuring what use we made of them.
   We never valued this poor seat of England;
   And therefore, living hence, did give ourself
   To barbarous licence; as 'tis ever common
   That men are merriest when they are from home.

4. But tell the Dauphin I will keep my state,
   Be like a king and show my sail of greatness
   When I do rouse me in my throne of France:
   For that I have laid by my majesty
   And plodded like a man for working-days,
   But I will rise there with so full a glory
   That I will dazzle all the eyes of France,
   Yea, strike the Dauphin blind to look on us.

5. And tell the pleasant prince this mock of his
   Hath turn'd his balls to gun-stones; and his soul
   Shall stand sore charged for the wasteful vengeance
   That shall fly with them:

6. for many a thousand widows
   Shall this his mock mock out of their dear husbands;

Mock mothers from their sons, mock castles down;
And some are yet ungotten and unborn
That shall have cause to curse the Dauphin's scorn.

7. But this lies all within the will of God,
   To whom I do appeal; and in whose name

8. Tell you the Dauphin I am coming on,
   To venge me as I may and to put forth
   My rightful hand in a well-hallow'd cause.

9. So get you hence in peace; and tell the Dauphin
   His jest will savour but of shallow wit,
   When thousands weep more than did laugh at it.
   Convey them with safe conduct. Fare you well.

We are glad the Dauphin is so pleasant with us!

Now consider the list of points below: these detail information about Henry that can be identified or strongly deduced from the text. Match them to the corresponding numbered sections and observe just how much source material about the man is provided by Shakespeare, all achieved in parallel with an incredibly dramatic and poetic piece of writing. Be aware that the context of the speech is all-important and that some of the information to be gathered can only be done so with reference to and knowledge of other parts of the play – in other words, there is a cumulative effect of detail. However, all you need to know in particular here is that the messenger has delivered the highly sarcastic gift of tennis balls from his master.

1. Henry is polite, courteous and able to conduct himself with formality and dignity. He is able to control his temper and not react in the way the Dauphin may have hoped and expected of him. He is a fine leader and statesman.

2. He can calmly, and with extreme control, make his point and state his intentions with frightening clarity and using imaginative inspiring use of metaphor and wordplay. He is extremely intelligent and well-educated.

3. He not only has honest self-knowledge about his riotous past youth, but is also aware of the opinion others have formed of him because of it. However, he is not concerned about this as he knows that he has changed and that his critics will soon be forced to change their minds about him. He is confident, self-aware and honest.

4. He is now every inch the king, a formidable warrior and a worthy leader of a strong

and powerful nation. He is ready to deal with his enemies, and the enemies of his country, swiftly, effectively and without mercy.

5. He has a dry sense of humour and can use words wittily, poetically and with rhythmic verve.

6. He is fully prepared to be ruthless when he needs to be and when the cause is just. He has faith and belief in his own righteousness and the guilt and blame of his enemies. He is not, in any sense, a moral or philosophical ditherer.

7. He has a fundamental and unswerving belief in God and he is unquestionably assured that He is on his side.

8. He has a strong sense of honour and of righteousness and will fight to the end to preserve it.

9. He is kind, fair and reasonable. He will show courtesy at all times and not stoop to ill-treating or even disrespecting those of a lower class and, in particular, the underlings of his enemies. However, he is very capable, within this, of straight-talking and unequivocal directness.

It is interesting to note that not only is there an incredible amount of information about character here but furthermore that information is exceedingly relevant to the themes of the play and Henry's place within it. Having recently become king, he is haunted by his past and the image of wasteful 'no-good' that his hard drinking and irresponsible younger years have cultivated. He is acutely aware that many believe that he is not fit to be king and he is utterly determined to prove them wrong. He views his future as one of strength, honour and righteous endeavour, and he cast aside his old ways (and friends) in order to become absolutely the man he believes he should be and fulfil the onerous duty that he believes to be his destiny.

There is nothing really within the speech regarding Henry's physical appearance, but there are several highly reasonable, direct and secure inferences that can be drawn about this from the content.

a. He is a well-built man, physically strong and imposing.

b. He is upright and proud of bearing – rising up to his full height.

c. He moves with authority, poise and dynamic energy.

d. His voice is confident, calm, well-modulated and strong.

e. His eye contact is firm, focused and open.

f. He dresses with appropriate dignity but wears his clothes with style.

g. His gesture is economical but large and passionate when used.

h. He physically owns and commands 'the space' – he is the physical focal point of every moment of the scene.

Part 2

You should now look at a short and edited extract of a scene from another play. The focus character for the exercise is not actually in the scene but is being spoken about. The scene is from Act I, scene iv, of *Antony and Cleopatra* and contains a conversation regarding Antony. It is numerated into 'point' sections once again.

Octavius: 1. *You may see, Lepidus, and henceforth know,*

It is not Caesar's natural vice to hate

Our great competitor: from Alexandria
This is the news:
2. he fishes, drinks, and wastes
The lamps of night in revel; is not more man-like
Than Cleopatra; nor the queen of Ptolemy
More womanly than he; hardly gave audience, or
Vouchsafed to think he had partners: you shall
   find there
A man who is the abstract of all faults
That all men follow.

Lepidus: I must not think there are
Evils enow to darken all his goodness:
3. His faults in him seem as the spots of heaven,
More fiery by night's blackness; hereditary,
Rather than purchased; what he cannot change,
Than what he chooses.

Octavius: 4. You are too indulgent. Let us
   grant, it is not
Amiss to tumble on the bed of Ptolemy;
To give a kingdom for a mirth; to sit
And keep the turn of tippling with a slave;
To reel the streets at noon, and stand the buffet
With knaves that smell of sweat: say this
becomes him,—
As his composure must be rare indeed
Whom these things cannot blemish,—yet must
   Antony
No way excuse his soils, when we do bear
So great weight in his lightness. If he fill'd
His vacancy with his voluptuousness,
Full surfeits, and the dryness of his bones,
Call on him for't: **5.** but to confound such time,
That drums him from his sport, and speaks as
   loud
As his own state and ours,—'tis to be chid
As we rate boys, who, being mature in knowledge,
Pawn their experience to their present pleasure,
And so rebel to judgment.

Antony, leave thy lascivious wassails.
6. When thou once
Wast beaten from Modena, where thou slew'st
Hirtius and Pansa, consuls, at thy heel
Did famine follow; whom thou fought'st against,
Though daintily brought up, with patience more
Than savages could suffer:
7. thou didst drink
The stale of horses, and the gilded puddle
Which beasts would cough at: thy palate then did
   deign
The roughest berry on the rudest hedge;
Yea, like the stag, when snow the pasture sheets,
The barks of trees thou browsed'st; on the Alps
It is reported thou didst eat strange flesh,
Which some did die to look on: and all this—
It wounds thine honour that I speak it now—
Was borne so like a soldier, that thy cheek
So much as lank'd not.

Lepidus: 'Tis pity of him.

Octavius: 8. Let his shames quickly
Drive him to Rome: 'tis time we twain
Did show ourselves i' the field; and to that end
Assemble we immediate council: Pompey
Thrives in our idleness.

Lepidus: To-morrow, Caesar,
I shall be furnish'd to inform you rightly
Both what by sea and land I can be able
To front this present time.

Octavius: Till which encounter,
It is my business too. Farewell.

Lepidus: Farewell, my lord: what you shall
   know meantime
Of stirs abroad, I shall beseech you, sir,
To let me be partaker.

Octavius: *Doubt not, sir;*
I knew it for my bond.

Consider the following points – observing the information you can glean about Antony from the observations of these two other characters. Remember that, because this is a play, the author is using this scene as a specific device not only to elucidate how Antony and his actions are interpreted in light of the view point of other protagonists in the drama, but also to transmit objective detail about him too: in other words, a certain amount of truth about Antony is on offer as well as the other characters, courtesy of their possibly biased opinion.

You may see, Lepidus, and henceforth know.

1. Antony is seen as a great and worthy colleague and partner to men of high office, but one who may also perhaps pose a threat and be feared as a rival.
2. He is a man of passion and love of life. Able to cast aside his responsibilities at times and fully indulge himself in extravagant pleasure.
3. However, he is a great man – one whose faults pale in comparison to his virtues, and who can be excused his failings in the context of the fact that, aware of his qualities and reputation, he can choose and afford to live opposite to them for a while.
4. Antony is a great womanizer – attracted to, and able to attract, women of mystique and intrigue. He is a highly sexual and sensuous being.
5. He is not panicked or distracted by the enormity of his responsibilities.
6. He is an experienced and successful soldier and general. A formidable warrior, capable of winning the hardest and bloodiest of battles.
7. He is an extraordinary tough man – physically strong and able to endure hardship and pain.
8. He is a man of honour, predisposed to feel shame and to act upon it.

Again, these personality enlightenments begin to build a physical picture of Antony in the mind:

a. He is large, muscular and imposing.
b. He is energetic, quick physically expressive.
c. He is facially rugged – not old, but lined with experience.

Handy Hint 19

Casting and Role Selection

The gloriously detailed and wonderfully defined nature of Shakespeare's human creations can be a double-edged sword for an actor. Although there is great scope for the imaginary process of acting to take over where the writer leaves off and to develop, embellish, extend and enrich to the heart's content, there is not perhaps the same amount of room or leeway in terms of 'type' of character that may be present with lesser playwrights.

It has already been established that an actor must draw a character out of themself, and Shakespeare's sheer expertise in detailed and specific characterizations makes it far more difficult to play parts that are not within their type and range. Whereas a little bit of unusual and 'creative' casting may be possible in other plays – the actor adapting and stretching to fill the role credibly – this is far more difficult and potentially hazardous when it comes to the Bard.

Therefore you must be careful to play only the parts for which you are suitable in terms of both physical and emotional factors. There is nothing worse, for instance, than seeing a male actor play Lear too young or a female actor play Cleopatra without having yet acquired the maturity and emotional depth to do so. By the same token, an actor who is suitable to play the Fool in King Lear or the Porter in Macbeth, might not be suitable for Antony or Henry.

Be adventurous in your work by all means but be careful that you do not suffer the potentially disastrous effects of miscasting.

Rehearsing the Porter.

You can clearly see from this exercise how Shakespeare is so deftly accomplished, establishing and building a character even within scenes in which they do not appear or directly feature. There is a huge wealth of source material available to an actor in every part of every play, and all of it is easily accessible and usable – firing and feeding the imagination and facilitating (although not guaranteeing) wonderfully realistic characterizations.

BUILDING A SHAKESPEAREAN CHARACTER

By now the starting point for your work on any character from any of Shakespeare's plays should be obvious. It should be equally evident that there is a vast wealth of information and resources for you to call upon from the text. Therefore, your first task, when approaching a characterization for the first time, should always be to study the play locating, examining and cataloguing all of the detail that is available to you there.

One of the biggest mistakes many actors make is to commence rehearsals without having sufficiently read, re-read and evaluated the play. This puts them at a disadvantage, whatever the playwright, but when it comes to Shakespeare the problem becomes serious. There is so much within the plays that an actor needs to make personal sense of before beginning to work with others (all with their own reactions and opinions) that a goodly proportion of preparatory time must be invested. This is particularly true in terms of the character that is to be portrayed: just as it is true that there is much information to be discovered, so it is also true that such amounts of detail will take considerable time and effort to locate and properly assimilate.

The best practical start that you can make to your private study of building a Shakespearean character is to actually list down upon a piece of paper, or in the margins of your script, all of the information about the character in question that you can find. It may also help to underline relevant lines and passages in your script too. Do not worry about being selective – note down anything that you believe to be relevant and helpful. As you have discovered in the exercises, some of this detail will be spoken by the character themselves and some by others about them. The latter will, of course, be in the context of personal relationships within the play and may be biased but do not be concerned by this – it is not a court of

law and the information you compile will be sifted by your own personal interpretational skills anyway.

IMAGINATION TIME

Having completed this initial process to the best of your ability, it is now time to begin fleshing-out the character in your own mind and by courtesy of your imaginative powers. Certainly, this will not be as arduous a task with Shakespeare in charge as it might otherwise be, but Shakespeare, like all good playwrights, does not deny the actor their considerable input – in fact he positively encourages it.

It may help you in this to continue your written list of information about the character, moving now in to full inventory mode. The kind of detail that you should be wishing to complete need not be of a self-indulgent and useless kind – such as 'what they had for breakfast' – but important and potentially relevant aspects of their lives that are not directly referred to in the play. Try to make sure that all of your imaginings are in keeping with, and faithful to, the stated information that you have already discovered. The dramatic process should be fully inclusive of an actor's contributions, and no playwright worth mentioning should be precious about any developments that practitioners instigate – provided (and this is a very big 'provided') that they keep within reasonable bounds of relevance to the play as a whole and the character as portrayed in the script in particular.

In developing your perception and understanding of the character, think about such things as their social status, family background, romantic lives, religious views,

---

Handy Hint 20

A Potential Problem

One of the mental barriers actors encounter when they are using their imaginations to develop character definitions and detail, is that of finding a Shakespearean character difficult to relate to personally. It is perceived that these people are inhabiting a fictitious world that is far removed in terms of time and location – with distant periods of history covered and vast, remote and exotic lands for locations. The huge and all-consuming moral dilemmas that they face can also seem far removed from the more mundane elements of 'real life'.

Essentially this is not a real problem at all (in fact quite the reverse) but is simply a matter of perception. Shakespeare is crammed full with modern relevancies – that is one of the main reasons he has so successfully survived the test of time. However, a present production of one of his plays has to interpret this relevance in a context that is accessible to a twenty-first century audience. That is why so many successful productions set the action of a play in a particular time, place and situation – not to be 'clever', but to make sense of and interpret a work of genius that is essentially timeless.

When working upon a character prior to rehearsals, or for personal study, you must find this context for yourself. Therefore, it may help to visualize any character that you may be studying in a very particular way. For instance, when working upon Henry or Cleopatra, rather than thinking of them as a remote king from English history or an exotic Egyptian queen, consider them as an ambitious young executive, taking over a large company after the retirement of his father, and a powerful woman heading-up some male-dominated organization, such as the police force or army. As long as the context you choose is relevant and faithful to the concepts of the play, this translating of circumstance will enable you to relate to the character more fully.

---

political allegiances, domestic situation, personal idiosyncrasies, opinions, likes, dislikes, prejudices and demeanour.

As Shakespeare's plays are thematically full of the important and grandiose aspects of human existence, it will also be important for you to think also about your character's morality, their attitude to good and evil, their philosophies, their passions and, perhaps most importantly of all, their relationship and attitude to the play's central themes – but more of that later.

You should not, at this stage, be concerned at all with the physical and vocal qualities of the character. This does not mean to say that

you will not begin to form a picture of them in your mind – or this is an inevitable side-effect of the work you are undertaking – but do not think at all now about how you will make this character move and speak. This will come later and, for the present, you must avoid making too early a decision about physicality, as this must come organically from your knowledge of the character once it is more fully formed.

It will also help not to allow your mental picture to become too fully formed. Try to keep it vague and do not place any importance upon it at all. Remember that it is you (your body, your voice) that must eventually give this character life: a disembodied picture of some idealized concept of characterization might prove a disadvantage when you have to become more practical and realistic later. For instance, visualizing Antony in all his masculine, rugged and intimidating glory may not be totally attainable when it comes to the final outcome. In other words, try at this early stage to work as much as possible from inside to out – and concentrate at present very much upon the 'inside' of your character.

EXERCISE – FINDING THE CHARACTER IN YOUR MIND

If you have not done so already, you should now practise formally your ability to develop knowledge of a character imaginatively, fictitiously and, above all, relevantly in another exercise.

Return to the character that you selected for the exercise 'Finding the Character on the Page' (*see* page 106) and revisit the copious notes that you made detailing information to be discovered about them from the text. Read these notes through very carefully in order to remind yourself of your findings.

If it is some time since you completed the exercise, re-read the play – this is never a waste of time as each reading of such extraordinary works will reveal and elucidate more and more for you.

Write the heading 'Additional Physical and Personality Characteristics' at the top of the third column. Write as many facts in this column that your imagination can supply. Make sure that these are not just re-writings of information you have already gleaned from the play, but new and different details that are totally personal to your image of the character and that are exclusively from your own

Find a modern context.

creativity. Do not stop until you have exhausted every idea you think is possible.

After a significant gap (perhaps the next day) return to the list and write some more – the break will almost certainly have revitalized your imagination.

If you find this exercise difficult, or feel that you can only supply a limited number of imaginings, use the lists in the first two columns of your paper from the original exercise. Take each fact and try to develop it – consider what other fact might be born of the original or what might be reasonable parallel conclusions to be drawn from them. Use each detail on the list as a starting place for further information and you may well find that this structure of working frees up your creative juices nicely.

THE CHARACTER'S RELATIONSHIP TO 'THEME'

There is one more important factor that you must consider while still at the stage of a cerebral understanding of character and prior to moving on to more physically active work. Shakespeare's plays have great themes of human experience and endeavour; in fact there are not many issues that he does not tackle or emotional dilemmas that he does not visit. For this reason you must involve yourself in the intellectual process of examining these themes and deciding how your character's journey through the play develops and expands

them. This will, of course, be most applicable to the major characters (especially to the eponymous heroes) but, being works of such quality and depth, you might be surprised as the extent that the smaller roles encompass the meaning and intentions of the playwright.

This is one of the most exciting areas of work that any actor has to be involved in, for it directly necessitates the use of personal opinion and viewpoint. It is important though that you do not unintentionally side-step the process by accepting or assuming that other people's analysis of the play in question is correct. There are countless books about what the plays mean and what Shakespeare was trying to communicate in writing them, but it is what you think that is vitally important, for it is you, and you alone, that must bring this character,

Screw your courage to the sticking place!

and the themes they carry, to life on this occasion.

You will also find that there are stock and bland preconceptions as to what the plays are about that might not be totally true or, at least, may not contain sufficient detail of truth for your purposes. Also, any such truth must be personal to you – it is your understanding of the play and your character's place within it that is required.

UNDERSTANDING MACBETH

A useful example to consider in this context is the character of Macbeth. It is a widely held view that Macbeth is a character involved in the moral dilemma of whether or not to murder Duncan in order to fulfil his ambitions, and that he is persuaded and cajoled into an act that he eventually regrets by his scheming and manipulative wife. While it would be untrue to say that this analysis is wrong, it is certainly fair to say that it is a massive over-simplification.

In fact, Macbeth is not really involved in a decision at all. He knows from the start that he will murder Duncan, for he knows that he is utterly compelled to fulfil the witches' prophesy that he will be king. His dilemma arises from the fact that he also knows for certain that in doing so he will be damned for eternity and that, after his inevitable eventual death, he will be bound straight for Hell with a one-way ticket. He teeters on the edge of a catastrophic course of action, analysing with great clarity the certainty of its consequences but unable to resist the elemental forces that pull him inevitably towards it. This is not a play about decision or moral temptation, it is a play about the power of evil and mankind's fight against it.

In contrast to Macbeth, Lady Macbeth seems to possess an all-pervading confidence and moral certainty of purpose. She chides her husband for what she sees as his lack of courage and strength. It is easy to assume, therefore, that she is the amoral, evil and unprincipled partner in this famous pairing. However, the main truth associated with her moral and philosophical character is that she, of the two, lacks the insight and depth of spiritual understanding that Macbeth possesses in spades. Once the deed has been committed, Macbeth has no need of regret or reparation as his perception of his situation was already formed – it is simply now too late and he accepts his eternal fate with alacrity and sets about easing his mortal passage to the grave, becoming an accomplished and vicious multi-murderer in the process.

When he sees the 'ghost' of Banquo, it is often assumed that he is suffering a malady of the mind induced by guilt and remorse. However, it is more enlightening of his character and beliefs to view this more as a horrifying affirmation of his certainty of damnation: it is a waking nightmare that will continue, in one form or another for the rest of eternity. One of the most dramatically significant factors about this is that Macbeth categorically knows his fate before he seals it – his fall is inevitable and irredeemable even before the act that propitiates it is committed.

Lady Macbeth, on the other hand, is totally unprepared for her journey towards judgement and justice, and she quickly loses her confidence and righteous poise in favour of self-doubt and eventual madness.

Of particular interest to an actor studying the characters of this great play are the reasons behind Macbeth's belief in destiny, evil and damnation. His world is one of superstition,

Will these hands ne'er be clean?

witchcraft and religious symbolism; it is also one of violence, battle and struggle. It is little wonder then that his relationship with the main themes of ambition, greed, power and evil is such a dramatic and inevitable one.

The Joy of Character Study

These musings about the play are, of course, an opinion or, more accurately, a particular reaction to the work. There are many possibilities of both differing and complementary theories and developments of idea and philosophy regarding *Macbeth* and this is one of the greatest plus points for any actor working

upon it or any other of Shakespeare's plays. It is this requirement to become involved in a character's moral, spiritual and emotional life in direct relationship to the themes of the play and their journey through it that marks out an artistic and cultural role for them to play in the process, rather than just one based upon entertainment and recreation.

This side of an actor's work is by far the best and most fulfilling, and when working on Shakespeare it is gloriously ever-present. However, if you have been used to more mundane acting tasks it is very important that you develop your thinking skills in regard to your character's place within the intellectual debates of the play. There is a two-fold way of operating here – one is your own personal ideas and understanding, the other is the communal consensus of the production and cast as a whole, of which you are an important part, but in terms of which you must be prepared to listen and parallel your views with those of others.

Debating a role and a play, either with yourself or others, is a habit which must be adopted and may require you to develop a more analytical mindset that you are used to or expect to need. As with all aspects of performance, it is a technique that can be learned, developed and honed.

Exercise – Exploring a Character Intellectually and Morally

If you are not familiar with the play *Othello*, obtain a copy (with good notes, of course) and read it thoroughly and carefully. Pay particular attention to the three main characters of Othello, Iago and Desdemona. Do not choose one of these roles in particular, as you will be considering them all equally within the exercise. Even if you are familiar with the play, a re-read will not do any harm.

Acquire some paper (or you may prefer to work with a notebook of some kind) and divide the pages into three columns, one for each character and head them appropriately.

For each of these three roles, make a list of all their qualities that you would regard as weaknesses. This is the most important starting point for any intellectual study of a character, as it is very often weakness that leads them towards the dilemmas that await them in the play.

When you have exhausted this list, draw a line beneath it in each column, and commence another list, this time of each character's strengths. You will probably find that this list is shorter for Iago than the other two (in the same way that Desdemona may have fewer weaknesses), but this does depend to a certain extent on how you interpret strength and you should remember that strength is not necessarily associated with goodness, in the same way that weakness does not have to be categorically bad in all instances.

The next part of your exploration is to examine how these two lists of strengths and weaknesses affect each character's journey through the moral fabric of the play in the particular light of their relationships and interactions with each other.

Draw lines between the columns, linking any strength or weakness of any of the three characters to any strength or weakness of any of the other two. In other words, if you feel one factor that you have noted has a bearing in any way upon another belonging to a different character (a strength being used against a weakness, for example) link them up. It doesn't matter how many lines you draw, or how many connections any particular factor makes with another.

Now consider any emotions or personal qualities (good and bad) that may be relevant to these linking strands. If you think, for instance, that any such factors as love, hate, rage, jealousy, trust, naivety, ambition, greed, purity, honesty, etc., played a part within the interpersonal relationships of the three characters, note them down by creating a small circle along the joining lines and writing the word within the circle. You may place any number of circles along each line.

Next, on a separate page, write an account made by each character, penned as if in their own words and as if after the events of the play, of how all of the links and circled words played a part in the circumstances and outcomes of the story and how their lives (and perhaps deaths) were affected by them. This should be, in effect, a personal interpretation and explanation, by each character, of the diagrammatic set of lists you have created. Remember that this is in retrospect and can show insights 'after the event'. Each character can also be analytical about the whole diagram and not just the factors that apply to them.

You may find it an interesting alternative to write your accounts in the form of letters written to each of the other characters. Either way, this and the other elements of the exercise should have really thrown up some stimulating debates about the themes of the play in your mind and helped to clarify and simplify the issues involved.

Finally, repeat this exercise using another Shakespeare play of your own choice, making

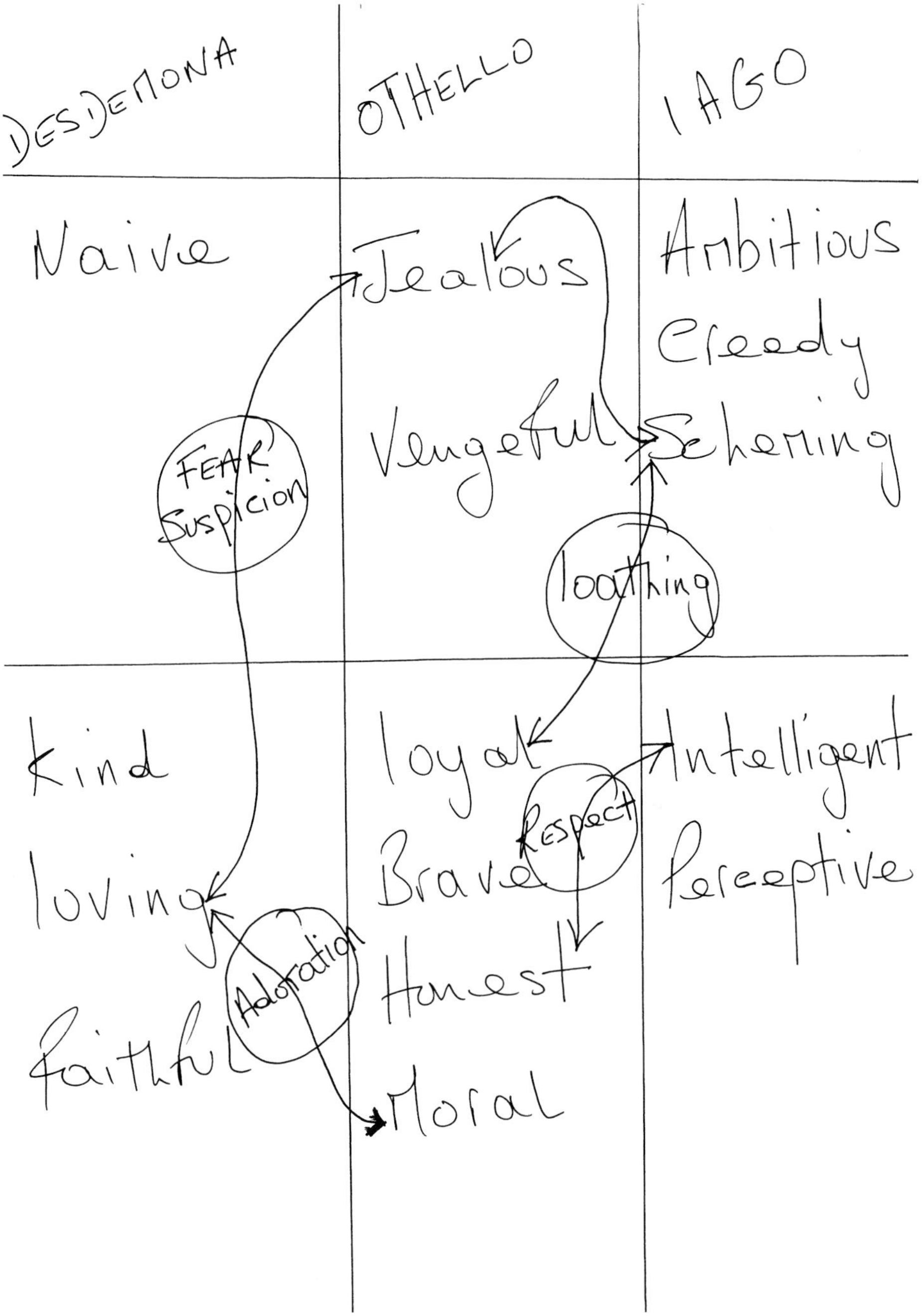

DESDEMONA	OTHELLO	IAGO
Naive	Jealous	Ambitious Greedy Scheming
	Vengeful	
Kind	loyal	Intelligent
loving	Brave	Perceptive
faithful	Honest	
	Moral	

FEAR Suspicion

loathing

Respect

Adoration

Interlinking strengths and weaknesses.

119

sure that you identify the main protagonists to include as your 'subjects' for the experiment.

CHARACTER MOTIVATION

On of the most defining aspects of any character in any play is what drives them – 'the desires and devices of their own hearts' and how these propel them dramatically through the play. Nowhere is this of more relevance and importance than in Shakespeare, for the simple reason that he deals with such grandiose and dramatic themes (as well as a plethora of more mundane, everyday and immediately identifiable ones) that the focus upon the motivations of the protagonists is obvious and critical.

There are two forms and degrees of motivation that actors must involve themselves with: the overall motivation that drives the character through the story (Macbeth's ambition being a pertinent example), and the smaller and more practical motivations that move them forwards through each scene – such as Iago trying to place a particular doubt in Othello's mind. There is, in fact, yet another layer of motivation that drives action itself – such as wanting to pick something up and thus moving towards it – but this is more appropriate to enabling spontaneity and co-ordination rather than character study itself.

Identifying the overall motivation of a character is, of course, reasonably straightforward, although even this may be open to personal

Lady Anne – complex motivations.

interpretation and is not always as simple or as baldly obvious as may appear. It may be argued, for example, that Macbeth is motivated not purely by simple and undefined ambition, but more specifically by an overwhelming sense of his own destiny and an irresistible desire to fulfil it at whatever cost.

EXERCISE – IDENTIFYING OVERALL MOTIVATION

Examine the following lists of female and male Shakespearean characters. Pick at least three of them, appropriate to your gender, and write down what you consider to be the overall motivation or motivations that are central to their journey through the play.

Female characters
Lady Macbeth in *Macbeth*
Rosalind in *As You Like It*
Imogen in *Cymbeline*
Portia in *The Merchant of Venice*
Katharina in *The Taming of the Shrew*
Viola in *Twelfth Night*
Lady Anne in *Richard the Third*
Juliet in *Romeo and Juliet*

Male characters
Demetrius in *A Midsummer Night's Dream*
Biron in *Love's Labour's Lost*
Benedick in *Much Ado About Nothing*
Hotspur in *Henry IV Part I*
Lear in *King Lear*
Hamlet in *Hamlet*
Benvolio in *Romeo and Juliet*

Handy Hint 21

Motivation – a Closer View

It is the various smaller and supporting motivations at scene level that are more difficult to identify and interpret. However, it is they that are the life blood of all Shakespearean characterization and engaging with them is an excellent way of approaching development of a character throughout a play.

It is very easy to forget and ignore the importance of motivation at this level. After all, human beings are not usually consciously aware of the nature and existence of such motivations as they go about their daily lives and it is easy, therefore, to underestimate their importance when it comes to characterization in drama. However, it is these basic and fundamental intentions that compose the engine that drives a scene and also the very framework upon which so much of characterization itself is based.

Much of drama is structured upon the various tensions and conflicts that exist between characters. These are, quite naturally, born of differing and opposing motivations and intentions and, without them, the drama would simply evaporate. What each character's motivations are depend, to a certain extent, upon the nature of their personalities but, as far as the actor is concerned, this can work in reverse, and a character may be personified and delineated by their motivations.

EXERCISE – IDENTIFYING MOTIVATION AT SCENE LEVEL

Look again at the scene from *Antony and Cleopatra* (Act I, scene iv) used for the exercise on page 108.

Work through the scene and note down what you think each character is trying to do in each of the eight numbered sections. Do not fall into the trap of being over-simplistic about this. Essentially, Octavius is trying to discredit Antony and Lepidus is trying to defend him and retain a good opinion of him. However, you will find, if you try, that you will be able to be more specific than this. For example, in Section 6, Octavius is attempting to influence Lepidus by flattering him and appealing to his ego.

You should be able to find a number of varying motivations for both characters as they converse through the scene.

Now read the scene through with a partner, and use the subtle changes in motivation to lead your acting through the scene. You will find that the very effort of always concentrating exactly on what you are trying to do at any given moment will enable your acting to be spontaneous and alive.

8 ENSEMBLE SHAKESPEARE

*Henry Goodman (Richard) with RSC artists in Richard III at
the Royal Shakespeare Theatre in Stratford-upon-Avon, 2003.
(Photo: Robbie Jack)*

BEING PART OF A TEAM

Acting is basically a team game. There is, of course, a limited number of plays written for just one performer but, by and large, drama concerns the interaction between a group of people; it is about tension and conflict between a certain and varying number of human beings in particular (and often extreme) situations.

Because of this, actors in a play have a huge dependency upon each other, and any one performer, however important the role they are playing may be, is totally reliant on fellow cast members for the quality of their performance. One of the most important facts that you can learn as an actor is this – you are only ever as good as the people that you are working with.

This is particularly true in Shakespearean productions. Although by now you should have discovered that performing the work of the Bard is not daunting, you will also know that it is certainly challenging. This is a challenge that cannot be met alone and the help, support and inspiration of your fellow performers will always remain essential.

Therefore, if until now you have been applying yourself to the work in this book alone, now is certainly the time to seek out fellow enthusiasts to work with.

LISTENING IN SHAKESPEARE

Acing is about the creation of a natural process in an unnatural situation. The natural process is that of bringing life, spontaneity and truth to a performance; the unnatural situation is the fact that you are doing this using words that have been written by somebody else – while a lot of other people are staring at you doing it!

In order for acting to be real it must be reactive. Even though you know what you are going to do next, and what you are going to say, you must do both of these things in a way that employs a natural process of interaction. The most important factor in attaining this is the necessity to really listen to what is being said to you (even though you know in advance what it will be) so that you can respond to it naturally and with appropriate spontaneity. Good acting stems from an ability to create real thoughts that then find expression in the real and organic expression of voice, gesture, facial expression and body posture. All of this must evolve from, and be centred around, listening – for in life many of our thoughts are motivated by what happens to us and are a reaction to communication we receive from others.

Until now, you have been concerned with what you have been doing and saying: now you must start to concentrate too on what is being done and said to you. Listening and reacting in a Shakespeare play may not be as instinctive as doing so in a modern piece. You have already discovered that unfamiliarity with the way Shakespeare uses language can lead to a perceived problem of understanding and you have countered this by stripping away the problem and finding the crystal clear and universally relevant meaning and intention that lies within the text.

However, so far you have done this focusing upon delivering this meaning clearly to an audience. Now is the time to realize that you need to deliver this meaning equally clearly to the fellow actors that you are talking to so that they can listen easily to what you are actually saying rather than the way that you are saying it. This, of course, works the other way round also: you must be able to receive clearly what is being given to you so that you may react to it spontaneously.

As with all acting and all drama, this is all about focusing upon not just what is being said but also the way it is being said; not to be blinded by the language but to be enlightened by the thought.

EXERCISE – LISTENING AND REACTING

Seek out a partner of the opposite sex for this exercise, as it will have no real value if studied alone. Make sure that you have read or re-read the play *Richard the Third*.

Lady, you know no rules of charity.

Start by just gently reading through the following scene together from Act I, scene ii. The dialogue is between Lady Anne and Gloucester (Richard) and contains the most marvellous interaction and interplay. Make sure, as ever, that you are using a copy of the text with good notes.

Duke of Gloucester: *Lady, you know no rules of charity,*
Which renders good for bad, blessings for curses.
Lady Anne: *Villain, thou know'st no law of God nor man:*
No beast so fierce but knows some touch of pity.
Duke of Gloucester: *But I know none, and therefore am no beast.*
Lady Anne: *O wonderful, when devils tell the truth!*
Duke of Gloucester: *More wonderful, when angels are so angry.*
Vouchsafe, divine perfection of a woman,
Of these supposed-evils, to give me leave,
By circumstance, but to acquit myself.
Lady Anne: *Vouchsafe, defused infection of a man,*
For these known evils, but to give me leave,
By circumstance, to curse thy cursed self.
Duke of Gloucester: *Fairer than tongue can name thee, let me have*
Some patient leisure to excuse myself.
Lady Anne: *Fouler than heart can think thee, thou canst make*
No excuse current, but to hang thyself.
Duke of Gloucester: *By such despair, I should accuse myself.*
Lady Anne: *And, by despairing, shouldst thou stand excused;*
For doing worthy vengeance on thyself,
Which didst unworthy slaughter upon others.
Duke of Gloucester: *Say that I slew them not?*

Lady Anne: *Why, then they are not dead:*
But dead they are, and devilish slave, by thee.
Duke of Gloucester: *I did not kill your husband.*
Lady Anne: *Why, then he is alive.*
Duke of Gloucester: *Nay, he is dead; and slain*
by Edward's hand.
Lady Anne: *In thy foul throat thou liest: Queen*
Margaret saw
Thy murderous falchion smoking in his blood;
The which thou once didst bend against her breast,
But that thy brothers beat aside the point.
Duke of Gloucester: *I was provoked by her*
slanderous tongue,
which laid their guilt upon my guiltless shoulders.
Lady Anne: *Thou wast provoked by thy bloody*
mind.
Which never dreamt on aught but butcheries:
Didst thou not kill this king?
Duke of Gloucester: *I grant ye.*
Lady Anne: *Dost grant me, hedgehog? then,*
God grant me too
Thou mayst be damned for that wicked deed!
O, he was gentle, mild, and virtuous!
Duke of Gloucester: *The fitter for the King of*
heaven, that hath him.
Lady Anne: *He is in heaven, where thou shalt*
never come.
Duke of Gloucester: *Let him thank me, that*
holp to send him thither;
For he was fitter for that place than earth.
Lady Anne: *And thou unfit for any place but*
hell.
Duke of Gloucester: *Yes, one place else, if you*
will hear me name it.
Lady Anne: *Some dungeon.*
Duke of Gloucester: *Your bed-chamber.*
Lady Anne: *I'll rest betide the chamber where*
thou liest!
Duke of Gloucester: *So will it, madam, till I*
lie with you.

Handy Hint 22

Trust your Colleagues

Now that you are moving into areas of study that necessitate you working with others, it is essential that you realize the vital importance of building and maintaining a strong relationship of trust and support.

Drama of every kind is all about taking risks and placing oneself, as a performer, in a highly exposed and vulnerable position. You cannot be a successful actor without taking these risks and, in order to do so, you must have absolute faith in your fellow company members.

Acting sometimes also requires physical and emotional intimacy. It is essential, therefore, that you work with people who are prepared to invest the same amount of commitment and devotion to the work as you are. You will not feel comfortable working with someone if you feel that they are holding back or not fully committing themselves to the process, and they will not feel comfortable working with you if they experience a similar reserve.

It is always worthwhile spending some time really getting to know new colleagues and playing a few trust games will prove a good investment of time and energy prior to beginning some serious work. Most important of all, make sure that you always respect others as they work, in the hope that they will extend the same level of respect to you.

Begin by discussing the scene together and ensuring that both of you understand what the scene is about and, most importantly, what each of you is trying to achieve in the scene. Identify the 'thrust and parry' between the two characters and make sure that you are both agreed on how the tension of the scene is structured and develops.

In your ruminations, concentrate on three main aspects that underpin the encounter. Firstly, Anne's anger and resentment towards Richard; secondly, his complete disregard to her sanctions and counter-determination to woo her in these most extraordinary circumstances; thirdly, and most vital to the success of the scene, the sexual tension, allied to the power struggle between them. With these three factors in mind, ensure that the actor playing Richard understands his incredible determination and completely uninhibited drive to fulfil his personal agenda, and that the actor playing Anne has, at least, some empathetic concept of the enormity of conflicting emotions that bombard her during the scene and how these emotions are born of, and feed off, each other. Only when you are sure that you have attained a very full and personally relevant understanding of the scene in terms of what it is about and your character's place within its structure and development, should you continue.

Now put aside your copies of the text, clear a space within the room you are working in, and simply improvise the scene or, more precisely, what happens in it. Forget Shakespeare's words while you are doing this and play the scene extempore, using your own words and modern idioms. Concentrate not upon the actual written development of the scene but rather what happens in it and the tension between the protagonists. You should find yourselves really beginning to strip away what is unnecessary in your thoughts and focusing upon the important factors within the encounter.

Repeat this improvisation several times,

stopping between attempts to discuss what is happening between you and what needs to be added or lost in order to attain a good parallel version of the written scene. While the mechanics of the relationship between the two characters must remain true to the text, the actual situation may be different – for example, they may be neighbours or the man may have been an ex-work colleague of his victim.

Next, pick up your scripts again so that you can repeat the improvisation once more but, this time, take each of the written speeches of each character in turn and play them in your own words. By doing this you will continue to explore your own version of the scene but you will be doing so within the rigidity of its original construction.

At this point in the process, you will now both not only know exactly what you are saying and doing and why, but you will also know exactly what is being said and done to you – or, at least, how your characters *perceive* what is being said and done to them. You will also be listening and reacting instinctively and automatically, for the very nature of improvisation demands this for it to succeed at all.

Now it is time to return to the text proper. Play the scene using Shakespeare's words and fully engage in the spirit of the scene's purpose. You should now find it very easy to actually listen to what is being said to you and allow your responses to be free and instinctive. Do not dwell upon the fact that you are acting Shakespeare, but that you are simply exchanging thoughts and intentions through his words. Structure your thoughts through the words and hear how your partner is doing exactly the same thing. You should be totally attuned to the thoughts of the scene rather than the language being used to convey them.

Play some trust games.

IMPROVISATION IS ESSENTIAL

The last exercise highlights the extraordinary usefulness of improvisation when ensemble working on a Shakespearean play. The importance of understanding (not intellectually or academically, but practically) can never be underestimated, and improvising is one of the quickest and most effective ways of achieving this understanding.

There are various ways that improvisation may be used as a tool. Sometimes, as with the previous exercise, it can elucidate what is actually happening in a scene by allowing the actors to play the scene's essential content without the encumbrance of text. At other times it may also be used to explore events which are not actually seen in the play itself but which have a bearing upon the action or the development of a character. For example, we do not witness Macbeth actually murdering Duncan but such is the importance of this act, not only upon the play's plot but the dramatic impetus of the scene that immediately follows it, that to improvise it in rehearsal may be of profound benefit.

However, it is important to remember that improvisation is not an alternative to the text but a servant to it. The point of working in this way is to find a better personal understanding of Shakespeare's work and not to change or supplant it.

It is also true that improvisation can be counter-productive if it is not used properly and with some thoughtful consideration. Do not just improvise for the sake of it but always ensure that you have a definite purpose in mind when you undertake it. Ensure that you and your colleagues are aware of why you are doing any particular improvisation and what it is that you hope it will achieve – the intended end result.

Improvisations can also go wrong and become silly and thus counter-productive. This is usually caused by a lack of structure and discipline within the work and so it is always helpful to be aware of a few basic rules of improvisation and to adhere to them.

* You should always 'accept and build' when improvising. That is, you should accept what another participant has said in contribution to the scene and build upon it if you can. In this way the work may go forward and not become stagnant, repetitive and pointless.

* You should always have a plan in your mind as to how the improvisation may progress, but you must remember and be sensitive to the fact that your fellow actors will also have ideas to contribute. The skill of extempore work is to find the balance between contributing and advancing your own ideas but being ready to adapt or perhaps abandon them altogether in the light of the input of your colleagues. You should be constantly aware of what is best for the scene as it develops and should not try to dominate

Improvisation should be focused and fun.

with your own concepts. However, you should be ready to advance these concepts and lead your fellows in pursuit of them if appropriate. The worse thing any actor can do in an improvisation is to 'sit on the sidelines' and leave the work to others.

* It is usually a good idea not to become too serious about an improvisation. By its very nature, this kind of work is informal and, to a certain extent, anarchic in nature – so have fun and use humour as much as is appropriate. Shakespeare is very structured – full of acts, scenes and words – so enjoy being free of this for a while so that you can discover what he is really all about.

* When working upon a 'prepared improvisation' – that is, one that has been discussed and perhaps rehearsed in advance prior to some sort of performance to an audience or other members of the rehearsal company – make sure that you structure the work properly and ensure that you have a strong beginning, middle and end, all focused towards the achievement required.

The following exercise is a random but appropriate improvisation to be undertaken by a group of actors working together and can be used to practise the 'rules of the game' while exploring Shakespeare at the same time.

Exercise – Improvising

In a group of around six to eight actors, each choose a well-known and important Shakespearean character, all from different plays.

The overall situation of the improvisation is that these characters are marooned on a desert island and must survive and coexist until rescue arrives.

Each character must behave and contribute to the situation in a manner wholly appropriate to their personality and the storyline in their own particular play. For instance, Macbeth will want to be the leader and try to dispose of anyone getting in his way (disposing need not mean literally murdering, as this is limiting to the potential story, it may just mean discrediting them with the others or making sure they become involved in an activity or task that distracts them from Macbeth's purposes). As another example, Katherina from *The Taming Of The Shrew* might berate the men and refuse to become involved in any domestic chores of survival.

Commence the improvisation and continue with it until action and development seem to have become exhausted or one character achieves some kind of dominance of victory over all the others.

Improvising with Text

Another reason why improvisation is so important in the process of rehearsing Shakespeare is that all acting should really be improvised, even when working with text in a script. This is because actors should move from moment to moment within the scene naturally, spontaneously and with a natural process of action and reaction, even though they already know the words they will say and the moves they will make. Indeed, the way a line is said will (and should) often vary from performance to performance because the impetus behind it will (and should) be 'improvised': the words and moves may remain constant but the 'acting' won't. Acting is a fluid thing: it is true improvisation, and especially when working with a playwright whose

Characters marooned.

work is so richly laden with words, it is essential that you maintain this.

Constant recourse to proper improvisation will help you enormously to achieve the same reality and naturalness when you return to the script. However, there is a way of actually working half way between the two when rehearsing: a kind of exercise that will help you to fully engage with the words and what they mean.

This is achieved by using an action or series of actions while speaking the lines which will help to focus the intentions and motivations behind them. Consider for a moment that you are working upon a scene, the content of which you are finding difficult to associate with or you are struggling to bring it alive with sufficient believability. Engaging in an appropriate action or activity as you play the scene can often liberate the acting within you and help you to find just the inspiration that you need. This is not to say that the action will remain in the final performance – although this has been known – but it is a simple and enjoyable way to free up your creativity in rehearsal.

There are numerous ways that this technique may manifest itself and only the imagination can limit the way it can be applied and the situations for which it may be used. The following examples will help you to understand how it works and can be applied.

* If you are working upon a scene of conflict between two people you might attempt to play the lines while trying to pull each other over a line drawn on the floor. Although the subsequent tone of your speaking may be too strained for the final version of the

scene, the experience should knock your articulation, breathing, energy and focus very firmly into the right gear.

* For a more subtle scene of conflict, for instance one where two protagonists are verbally sparring with each other in a quite shaded and less obvious way, it might help to speak the lines as you continually and purposefully move an object to different places on a table. Each speaker should insist that it be replaced where they want it to be and firmly move it there as they speak the words that reassert their dominance of the exchange.

* A scene of courtship, romance or flirting may be enhanced by the couple dancing during their dalliance together.

* Exuding menace could be facilitated by slowly circling the victim or carefully cleaning a knife whilst speaking.

* Misunderstanding and lack of communication between two opposite personalities encountering each other may be cemented by building a wall of chairs between them as they continue through the scene.

* A scene of reconciliation may be similarly served by building together a pile or sculpture made of said chairs.

One thing is certain, there are many and every types of human situation and confrontation to be found amongst the pages of Shakespeare and there is a multitude of possibilities for helping to understand, release and enliven them. Some of these exercises may actually serve the 'blocking' process itself and end up in the final performance of the play. Others will simply complete their purpose of allowing the actor to find the truth in what they are saying and doing.

Sometimes this exercise helps particularly by

Action aids text.

defusing the intensity of the speech into action: it acts a transference mechanism, allowing the actor to find a more balanced and appropriate way of speaking the text concerned.

It will help you now to experiment with this technique using a specific example from a play, with a possible problem in playing it and a specific idea to help solve it.

EXERCISE – IMPROVISING WITH THE TEXT

You will need to enlist the help of colleagues for this exercise and form a 'company' comprising one man and three women.

Read and absorb the following scene. It is an edited version from the very famous beginning

Handy Hint 23

Begin to Consolidate

Now that you have started to work with other people, albeit in an already established group or one that you have assembled specially, remember to put into practice all of the various elements you have learned so far.

As you work upon the exercises here, try also to experiment with the skills of voice, movement and characterization and begin the process of assimilating them into a whole that will eventually become your 'technique'.

The most important thing is to enjoy your new-found abilities – show off a bit and utilize your skills to the full. You will find now that everything will begin to connect and you will start to find that which seemed daunting now simply enjoyable and exhilarating.

of the plot of *King Lear* (Act I, scene i). In this scene the aging Lear has decided to divide his kingdom between his three daughters and, in contemplation of this task, asks each to declare how much they love him. Two of his daughters, Goneril and Regan, are fulsome in their declarations but steeped in insincerity and artifice. Cordelia, the third, youngest and most adored daughter, cannot and will not defile the love she has for her father with such self-serving and extravagant platitudes. She states her love simply, honestly and practically – emphasizing that her dedication to her father cannot be exclusive and must be extended to her future husband too. This enrages Lear, who is blind to the shallowness of his older daughters, and he disinherits Cordelia and banishes her from his sight.

Lear: Tell me, my daughters
(Since now we will divest us both of rule,
Interest of territory, cares of state),
Which of you shall we say doth love us most?
That we our largest bounty may extend
Where nature doth with merit challenge. Goneril,
Our eldest-born, speak first.
Goneril: Sir, I love you more than words can
   wield the matter;
Dearer than eyesight, space, and liberty;
Beyond what can be valued, rich or rare;
No less than life, with grace, health, beauty,
   honour;
As much as child e'er lov'd, or father found;
A love that makes breath poor, and speech unable.
Beyond all manner of so much I love you.
Lear: Of all these bounds, even from this line to
   this,
To thine and Albany's issue
Be this perpetual.– What says our second
   daughter,
Our dearest Regan, wife to Cornwall? Speak.
Regan: Sir, I am made
Of the selfsame metal that my sister is,
And prize me at her worth. In my true heart
I find she names my very deed of love;
Only she comes too short, that I profess
Myself an enemy to all other joys
Which the most precious square of sense possesses,
And find I am alone felicitate
In your dear Highness' love.
Lear: To thee and thine hereditary ever
Remain this ample third of our fair kingdom,
Now, our joy,
Although the last, not least; what can you say to
   draw
A third more opulent than your sisters? Speak.
Cordelia: Nothing, my lord.

Lear: *Nothing?*

Cordelia: *Nothing.*

Lear: *Nothing can come of nothing. Speak again.*

Cordelia: *Unhappy that I am, I cannot heave*
My heart into my mouth. I love your Majesty
According to my bond; no more nor less.

Lear: *How, how, Cordelia? Mend your speech a*
little,
Lest it may mar your fortunes.

Cordelia: *Good my lord,*
You have begot me, bred me, lov'd me; I
Return those duties back as are right fit,
Obey you, love you, and most honour you.
Why have my sisters husbands, if they say
They love you all? Haply, when I shall wed,
That lord whose hand must take my plight shall
carry
Half my love with him, half my care and duty.
Sure I shall never marry like my sisters,
To love my father all.

Lear: *But goes thy heart with this?*

Cordelia: *Ay, good my lord.*

Lear: *So young, and so untender?*

Cordelia: *So young, my lord, and true.*

Lear: *Let it be so! thy truth then be thy dower!*

Suppose, for the sake of the exercise, that rehearsals of this scene are not working and you four, the cast, are experiencing three main problems.

1. The actors playing Goneril and Regan are finding it difficult to find the right level of exuberance in order to allow the audience to be aware of their insincerity while remaining plausible enough to Lear (albeit he an aging man) and the attending courtiers.
2. The actor playing Cordelia cannot properly play the opposite of their dishonesty with-out appearing cold and lacking in the real and very deep feelings of love that she does have for her father.
3. The actor playing Lear is having difficulty portraying the vestiges of a great and powerful man, whilst not being able to 'see through' his older daughters complicity, and changing his opinion of his most favoured daughter so drastically and rapidly in the face of such truthful testimony.

Whilst these problems are obviously contrived it is not inconceivable that they would arise in a genuine rehearsal process of the play and, in fact, these are the very issues that underpin the playing of the scene anyway and should be examined in rehearsal as a matter of course.

Attempt, in turn, the following three suggestions for ways in which to rehearse the scene. They contain action and movement designed as focusers of the emotional content of the scene and possible curatives of the potential problems.

1. At the beginning of the scene each of the three daughters should be carrying gifts. Goneril and Regan have several each and, as they speak their individual homilies, they should place them at the feet of an enthroned Lear. The gifts may be anything – boxes or objects found around the rehearsal room will suffice – for it is the symbolism that is important; but they should be as large as possible, signifying extravagance and excess. Cordelia should present one simple and un-elaborate gift which she places directly into Lear's hands.
2. Lear should start the scene in shirt sleeves and standing. During the progression of the scene, and as they speak, Goneril and

King Lear and his daughters.

Regan dress him – in a slow and ceremonious fashion – with jacket, cloak and hat (crown). Cordelia completes the process, during her speech, by gently dabbing his face clean with a moist cloth.

3. Lear should stand in the middle of the room with Goneril and Regan either side of him. They speak their speeches simultaneously, each trying to get his attention by pulling him physically around towards them and coercing him across to their side of the room. Cordelia, conversely, kneels before him as she speaks, without touching or cajoling him in any way.

9 A PRACTICAL EXAMPLE

Michael Maloney (Romeo) and Clare Holman (Juliet) in the RSC's Romeo and Juliet *at Stratford-upon-Avon, 1992. (Photo: Robbie Jack)*

This chapter contains a complete Shakespearean show. In effect it is made up of some extracts from various plays, loosely joined together by an imaginary concept. It is a blatant rewriting of history in which Shakespeare, down on his luck and out of a job, forms a new company from tramps that he meets on the streets and, in doing so, revitalizes both his plays and himself.

The play extracts have been chosen carefully to provide a challenging but entertaining selection for any company to work upon. The aim here is not only to provide a performance vehicle for you to rehearse but also to continue and extend the learning process. To this end there are extensive notes included in the second half of the chapter.

Therefore, even if you do not intend to perform these extracts, you should treat this chapter in exactly the same way as you have the others, reading it carefully and working upon it as usual. If you wish, you may apply the earlier exercises in the book to the extracts and use them to experiment with and develop your technique.

The casting of each extract is fluid and adaptable – allowing any tramp to play any part and giving you flexibility in the number of participants that are used.

DOWN AND OUT WITH BILL SHAKESPEARE

Scene 1
(The scene is the Shakespeares' living room. The telephone rings four times. The answering machine cuts in.)

Bill's Voice: Hello! This is a recorded message. I'm afraid William Shakespeare and Ann Hathaway are unable to take your call at present, but if you would like to leave your name, number and a short message, we will get back to you just as soon as we can. Thank you for calling. Please speak after the tone.

(Bill enters. He looks tired and dishevelled. He pours himself a large drink and sits in an old, badly worn armchair. He presses the button on his phone for messages.)

(Bleep.)

Ben's Voice: Hello Billy darling! It's Ben speaking – Ben Jonson. Just to let you know how dreadfully sorry I was to read those awful

Down and Out with Bill Shakespeare.

137

reviews. How absolutely hideous for you, my dear! I mean, you may be past your prime, but the show's not quite as bad as they make out. Love to Ann. Bye!

(Bleep.)

Jim's Voice: Hi Bill! It's James Burbage. Look, I've been trying to get hold of you all over the place. I must speak to you as soon as poss. I tried your mobile but there was no reply. Things are looking bad old mate. These reviews have been the last straw. The bookings are practically non-existent beyond this week. Anyway, I've had a couple of reasonable offers for the Globe. So please, please give me a bell. I want to talk to you before I take the final decision. Speak to you soon.

(Bleep.)

Ann's Voice: Hello William! It's Ann. I'm at Mother's. I'm not coming back. I'm sorry, darling, I just can't take any more. There's not much in the freezer I'm afraid – you haven't given me any housekeeping for weeks. There's some of that boar's head left over from Sunday in the fridge. And do try to pay these bills – they're all final demands you know. Well, take care of yourself. Goodbye!

(Bleep.)

Jim's Voice: Bill! It's James, again. Bad news – I had to sell. Sorry, mate, but I waited to hear from you as long as I could. I've cleared your desk for you – put it all in a cardboard box. I'll keep hold of it until I see you. Never mind, eh! I put it down to the recession. Who knows, another time, another place – we might have

made it. Keep in touch and good luck for the future. Love to Ann. Bye.

Scene 2
(The scene changes to a street somewhere in London. Bill enters. He places a crate on the ground with his cap with a few coins already in it on the ground. He stands on the crate and clears his throat.)

Bill: Shall I compare thee to a summer's day?
Thou art more lovely and more temperate.
Rough winds do shake the darling buds of May,
And summer's lease hath all too short a ....

Shall I compare thee to a summer's day?

(As he speaks he has attracted the attention of several vagrants.)

Tramp 1: Hey, you! What the hell do you think you're doing?
Bill: I'm sorry, were you addressing me?
Tramp 1: That's right! Who are you?
Bill: My good woman, I am the world famous playwright – William Shakespeare.
Tramp 2: Never heard of you!
Tramp 3: I have – you're the bloke who's just gone bust.

(Bill steps off his crate.)

Bill: I have sustained a slight financial set-back, yes.
Tramp 2: Is that why you're busking then?
Bill: I would prefer to call it One Man Street Theatre.
Tramp 3: Oh, very *Time Out*!
Tramp 4: What happened to your posh the-atre and your arty-farty actors then?
Bill: I've moved on from there, to a more grass roots type of presentation.
Tramp 1: Cobblers!! You're skint!
Tramp 4: We'll be your actors – you won't get more grass roots than us. Teach us some of your plays. Or don't you think we'd be able to understand them?
Bill: My dear friend, my plays were written for the common man – but I hardly think that ....
Tramp 2: Tell us 'common men'....
Tramp 1: And women!
Tramp 2: ... about some of them.
Bill: Very well, if you insist! *Henry the Fifth*, for example. Ostensibly, the story of a newly crowned king's brilliant leadership in defeat-ing the French, but also of the rejection of his old working class friends from the days of his reckless youth: friends who, though hurt and confused by his seeming indifference to them, are still ready and willing to rally to the call of war in support of this great King – Henry!

(The tramps pick up broom handles, dustbin lids and other pieces of street debris. They brandish them as they surround Bill, chanting supportively).

Tramps: Henry! Henry! Henry! Henry!

(Bill hesitates reluctantly then, making up his mind, he jumps back upon the crate and becomes Henry the Fifth.)

Tramps: Hooray!
Henry: Once more unto the breach, dear
    friends, once more;
Or close the wall up with our English dead.
Tramps: Hooray!
Henry: In peace there's nothing so becomes a
    man
As modest stillness and humility:
But when the blast of war blows in our
    ears,
Then imitate the action of the tiger;
Stiffen the sinews, summon up the blood,
Disguise fair nature with hard-favour'd
    rage;
Then lend the eye a terrible aspect;
Let pry through the portage of the head
Like the brass cannon; let the brow o'er
    whelm it
As fearfully as doth a galled rock
O'erhang and jutty his confounded base,
Swill'd with the wild and wasteful ocean.
Tramps: Hooray!
Henry: Now set the teeth and stretch the
    nostril wide,

Hold hard the breath and bend up every
    spirit
To his full height. On, on, you noblest
    English.
Tramps: Hooray!
Tramp 1: We're with you, Harry!
Henry: Whose blood is fet from fathers of
    war-proof!
Fathers that, like so many Alexanders,
Have in these parts from morn till even
    fought
And sheathed their swords for lack of
    argument:
Dishonour not your mothers; now attest
That those whom you call'd fathers did
    beget you.
Be copy now to men of grosser blood,
And teach them how to war.
Tramps: Fight! Fight! Fight! Fight!
Henry: And you, good yeoman....
Tramps: Yes?
Henry: Whose limbs were made in England,
    show us here
The mettle of your pasture; let us swear
That you are worth your breeding; which I
    doubt not;
Tramps: Yes!
Henry: For there is none of you so mean
    and base,
That hath not noble lustre in your eyes.
I see you stand like greyhounds in the slips,
Straining upon the start.
Tramps: Hooray!
Henry: The game's afoot:
Follow your spirit, and upon this charge
Cry 'God for Harry, England, and Saint
    George!'
Tramps: Hooray!

(The tramps shoulder William off the crate and

Handy Hint 24

Keep It Simple

If you decide to stage your own Shakespearean production, whether it be an entire play or a construction of extracts like Down and Out with Bill Shakespeare, do not make life too difficult for yourself in terms of scenery, costumes and props.

It is sometimes appropriate to use basic costume for the whole ensemble – such as blacks or, in this case, scruffy clothing – and then have simple pieces of costume to put over this for the various characters as they are played.

You can take the same attitude to props – using everyday items that are 'appropriate' for what they represent rather than authentic.

Above all, do not stretch your resources beyond your time and budget: keep it simple and concentrate upon the story, acting and text. Shakespeare should be brought alive with humanity, not elaboration and excess.

---

carry him triumphantly off-stage, picking-up and continuing their chant as they do so.)

Tramps: Henry! Henry! Henry! Henry!

Scene 3
(Bill returns to the stage, carrying a celebratory bottle of beer. The tramps return behind him, setting-up the next scene using more crates and casks as furniture. Bill speaks directly to the audience.)

Bill: And so it seemed I had a new company. Not quite as so 'polished' perhaps as before, but certainly less precious and temperamental and, at last, I had some women!

Tramp 1: I should think so too!

Bill: We began to rehearse our repertoire – beginning with a haunting scene from *Henry the Fifth.*

(For this, as for all the following extracts, the tramps play the various parts as required and appropriate.)

Hostess Quickly: Prithee, honey-sweet husband, let me bring thee to Staines.

Pistol: No; for my manly heart doth yearn.
Bardolph, be blithe: Nym, rouse thy vaunting
    veins:
Boy, bristle thy courage up; for Falstaff he is
    dead,
And we must yearn therefore.

Bardolph: Would I were with him,
    wheresome'er he is, either in
heaven or in hell!

(The characters freeze.)

Bill: My new cast soon found exactly the right tone for this scene, in which they mourn the passing of one of the most exuberant characters in any of my plays – Falstaff.

(They un-freeze.)

Hostess Quickly: Nay, sure, he's not in hell:
    he's in Arthur's
bosom, if ever man went to Arthur's bosom.
    A' made
a finer end and went away an it had been any
christom child; a' parted even just between
    twelve
and one, even at the turning o' the tide: for
    after
I saw him fumble with the sheets and play with

flowers and smile upon his fingers' ends, I
    knew
there was but one way; for his nose was as
    sharp as
a pen, and a' babbled of green fields. 'How
    now,
Sir John!' quoth I. 'what, man! be o' good
cheer.' So a' cried out 'God, God, God!' three or
four times. Now I, to comfort him, bid him a'
should not think of God; I hoped there was no
    need
to trouble himself with any such thoughts
    yet. So
a' bade me lay more clothes on his feet: I put my
hand into the bed and felt them, and they
    were as
cold as any stone; then I felt to his knees, and
they were as cold as any stone, and so upward
    and
upward, and all was as cold as any stone.

Nym: They say he cried out of sack.

Hostess Quickly: Ay, that a' did.

Bardolph: And of women.

Hostess Quickly: Nay, that a' did not.

Boy: Yes, that a' did; and said they were devils
incarnate.

Hostess Quickly: A' could never abide
    carnation; 'twas a colour he
never liked.

Boy: A' said once, the devil would have him
about women.

Hostess Quickly: A' did in some sort, indeed,
    handle women; but then
he was rheumatic, and talked of the whore of
    Babylon.

Boy: Do you not remember, a' saw a flea stick
    upon
Bardolph's nose, and a' said it was a black soul
burning in hell-fire?

Bardolph: Well, the fuel is gone that

maintained that fire:
that's all the riches I got in his service.

(The characters freeze.)

Bill: In order for my actors to fully appreciate the poignant nature of this scene, I had to tell them that the characters sombre mood is much increased by their old drinking and carousing companion's rejection of them since he became king. A rejection that they, as good working class subjects, did not reciprocate when asked to follow him to war.

(They un-freeze.)

Nym: Shall we shog? the king will be gone from
Southampton.
Pistol: Come, let's away. My love, give me thy lips.
Look to my chattels and my movables:
Let senses rule; the word is 'Pitch and Pay:'
Trust none;
For oaths are straws, men's faiths are wafer-cakes,
And hold-fast is the only dog, my duck:
Therefore, Caveto be thy counsellor.
Go, clear thy crystals. Yoke-fellows in arms,
Let us to France; like horse-leeches, my boys,
To suck, to suck, the very blood to suck!
Boy: And that's but unwholesome food they say.
Pistol: Touch her soft mouth, and march.
Bardolph: *(Kissing her)* Farewell, hostess.
Nym: I cannot kiss, that is the humour of it; but, adieu.
Pistol: Let housewifery appear: keep close, I thee command.
Hostess Quickly: Farewell; adieu.

Scene 4
(The tramps re-set the scene as Bill continues to narrate to the audience.)

Bill: In order to keep their interest, I decided that my ragbag of performers should next tackle some comedy. The scene I gave them, even though I say so myself, is probably one of my funniest. It comes from *As You Like It* – and they liked it!

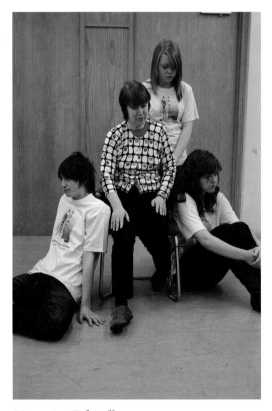

Mourning Falstaff.

Touchstone: Come apace, good Audrey; I will fetch up your goats, Audrey. And how, Audrey, am I the man yet? Doth my simple feature content you?

Audrey: Your features! Lord warrant us! What features?

Touchstone: I am here with thee and thy goats, as the most
capricious poet, honest Ovid, was among the Goths.

Jaques: *(Aside)* O knowledge ill-inhabited, worse than Jove in a
thatch'd house!

(The characters freeze.)

Bill: My actors lapped up the chance to play the hilariously dim-witted Audrey and her long-suffering but practical 'Clown' of a suitor, Touchstone. And there was fierce competition amongst the men as to who should play the dry, worldly and gloriously sardonic commentator upon life, Jaques.

(The actors un-freeze and cheekily acknowledge the audience as they are mentioned.)

Touchstone: When a man's verses cannot be understood, nor a man's
good wit seconded with the forward child understanding, it
strikes a man more dead than a great reckoning in a little room.
Truly, I would the gods had made thee poetical.

Audrey: I do not know what 'poetical' is. Is it honest in deed and
word? Is it a true thing?

Touchstone: No, truly; for the truest poetry is the most feigning,
and lovers are given to poetry; and what they swear in poetry may
be said as lovers they do feign.

Audrey: Do you wish, then, that the gods had made me poetical?

Touchstone: I do, truly, for thou swear'st to me thou art honest;
now, if thou wert a poet, I might have some hope thou didst
feign.

Audrey: Would you not have me honest?

Touchstone: No, truly, unless thou wert hard-favour'd; for honesty
coupled to beauty is to have honey a sauce to sugar.

Jaques: *(Aside)* A material fool!

Audrey: Well, I am not fair; and therefore I pray the gods make me
honest.

Touchstone: Truly, and to cast away honesty upon a foul slut were
to put good meat into an unclean dish.

Audrey: I am not a slut, though I thank the gods I am foul.

Touchstone: Well, praised be the gods for thy foulness;
sluttishness may come hereafter.

(The characters freeze.)

Bill: I couldn't have been prouder of these guys. The amount and quality of wordplay in the scene is amazing, even by my standards, and they coped with it like veterans. But no time to relax – there was more to come!

Touchstone: But be it as it may be, I will
marry thee; and to that end I have been with Sir Oliver Martext,
the vicar of the next village, who hath promis'd to meet me in
this place of the forest, and to couple us.

Jaques: *(Aside)* I would fain see this meeting.

Audrey: Well, the gods give us joy!

Touchstone: Amen. A man may, if he were

Come apace, good Audrey!

of a fearful heart, stagger
in this attempt; for here we have no temple
   but the wood, no
assembly but horn-beasts. But what though?
   Courage! As horns are
odious, they are necessary. It is said: 'Many a
   man knows no end
of his goods.' Right! Many a man has good
   horns and knows no end
of them. Well, that is the dowry of his wife;
   'tis none of his
own getting. Horns? Even so. Poor men alone?
   No, no; the noblest
deer hath them as huge as the rascal. Is the
   single man therefore
blessed? No; as a wall'd town is more worthier
   than a village, so

is the forehead of a married man more
   honourable than the bare
brow of a bachelor; and by how much
   defence is better than no
skill, by so much is horn more precious than
   to want.

Bill: Stand by – here comes one of my
favourites – the comedy vicar!

Touchstone: Here comes Sir Oliver.
(Enter SIR OLIVER MARTEXT)
Sir Oliver Martext, you are well met. Will you
   dispatch us here
under this tree, or shall we go with you to
   your chapel?
Sir Oliver Martext: Is there none here to

give the woman?

I will not take her on gift of any man.

Sir Oliver Martext: Truly, she must be given, or the marriage is not lawful.

Jaques: *(Discovering himself)* Proceed, proceed; I'll give her.

Touchstone: Good even, good Master What-ye-call't; how do you, sir?

You are very well met. Goddild you for your last company. I am

very glad to see you. Even a toy in hand here, sir. Nay; pray be

cover'd.

Jaques: Will you be married, motley?

Touchstone. As the ox hath his bow, sir, the horse his curb, and

the falcon her bells, so man hath his desires; and as pigeons

bill, so wedlock would be nibbling.

Jaques: And will you, being a man of your breeding, be married

under a bush, like a beggar? Get you to church and have a good

priest that can tell you what marriage is; this fellow will but

join you together as they join wainscot; then one of you will

prove a shrunk panel, and like green timber warp, warp.

Touchstone: *(Aside)* I am not in the mind but I were better to be

married of him than of another; for he is not like to marry me

well; and not being well married, it will be a good excuse for me

hereafter to leave my wife.

(The characters freeze.)

Bill: Touchstone's brilliantly logical but off-beat outlook on life produces a raised eyebrow from the quizzical Jaques.

(They un-freeze.)

Tramp Playing Jaques: Do you actually want me to do that?

Bill: What?

Tramp: Raise my eyebrow.

Bill: Of course not. I didn't mean literally.

Tramp: Didn't you?

Bill: No. I was being metaphorical. It's what I do. Now get on with it!

Jaques: Go thou with me, and let me counsel thee.

Handy Hint 25

A Workable Set

When you are performing Shakespeare, it will help you immensely if you are able to use a set that is flexible and adaptable. It need not be expensive or elaborate but, within your budget, should afford you the greatest possible fluidity of use.

Shakespeare plays all have many scenes, usually ranging across many different locations. Therefore, you will need a set that has various different spaces that can represent different places at different times. One of the best ways of achieving this is to use a set which has different levels, and this can often be reasonably simply achieved with the use of scaffolding.

Try to be as inventive as possible and remember that your ideas do not have to be complicated or expensive in order to be effective.

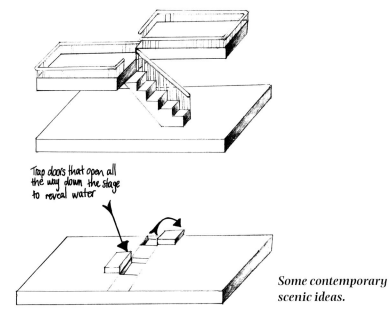

Trap doors that open all the way down the stage to reveal water

Some contemporary scenic ideas.

Touchstone. Come, sweet Audrey;
We must be married or we must live in bawdry.
Farewell, good Master Oliver. Not-
O sweet Oliver,
O brave Oliver,
Leave me not behind thee.
But- wind away, be-gone, I say,
I will not to wedding with thee.
(Exit JAQUES, TOUCHSTONE, and AUDREY)
Sir Oliver Martext. 'Tis no matter; ne'er a
    fantastical knave of them all
shall flout me out of my calling. *(Exit)*

Scene 5
(The tramps re-set the scene as Bill continues.)

Bill: By now we had finished rehearsals and were out and about performing, to great acclaim, an ever-changing selection of scenes under the umbrella title of *Bill's Best Bits.*
Tramp 2: *(Proudly)* I thought of that!
Bill: Our success continued as the street the-atre attracted ever larger audiences. Then came the break I was really looking for – a paid booking. We were to be top of the bill at *The Olde Stratford Working Men's Club.* OK, admit-tedly not the centre of the cultural and intellectual universe, but an important venue nonetheless.
Tramp 3: And great pies!
Chairman: *(With microphone)* Four and two – forty two. Six and eight – sixty eight. Two little ducks....
Tramps: Quack, Quack!
Chairman: ....twenty two.
Tramp 3: House!
Chairman: We have a winner, ladies and gentlemen – and what a lovely lady she is!

(Tramp 3, who is a man, mimics a coy female.)

Chairman: She's won tonight's star prize – a voucher for a half-price shampoo and set at Lorenzo's in the high street.

146

Showtime!

(Tramp 3 feigns excitement as the others applaud.)

Chairman: Before the 'turn' comes on, I have a message from the janitor: would the person who removed the ladder from the storeroom please return it or further steps will be taken. *(Laughter.)* And now ladies and gentlemen, it's the moment you've all been waiting for – tonight's cabaret. Unfortunately, for those of you who were looking forward to seeing Stanley Bennett and his performing ferret, Stanley has had to cancel because the ferret's ill. *(Sympathetic sounds.)* But instead, and at great expense, we have for you a bit of culture.

(Impressed sounds.) Fresh from their recent performances on the streets of London, we proudly present *Mr Bill Shakespeare and his Down and Out Players. (Applause.)*

Bill: The show was a fantastic success. The audience loved it. And then came the big and exciting ending – an extract from my thriller, *Macbeth*. A distorted and perverted story of love, power, greed and ambition – a loyal subject driven by elemental forces to murder his King – a tale of deep emotions set against the eerie backdrop of a dark and brooding castle – I just knew it was going to go down a storm!

Macbeth. If it were done when 'tis done, then 'twere well
It were done quickly: if the assassination
Could trammel up the consequence, and catch
With his surcease success; that but this blow
Might be the be-all and the end-all here,
But here, upon this bank and shoal of time,
We'd jump the life to come. But in these cases
We still have judgment here; that we but teach
Bloody instructions, which, being taught, return
To plague the inventor: this even-handed justice
Commends the ingredients of our poison'd chalice
To our own lips. He's here in double trust;
First, as I am his kinsman and his subject,
Strong both against the deed; then, as his host,
Who should against his murderer shut the door,
Not bear the knife myself. Besides, this

Duncan
Hath borne his faculties so meek, hath been
So clear in his great office, that his virtues
Will plead like angels, trumpet-tongued, against
The deep damnation of his taking-off;
And pity, like a naked new-born babe,
Striding the blast, or heaven's cherubim, horsed
Upon the sightless couriers of the air,
Shall blow the horrid deed in every eye,
That tears shall drown the wind. I have no spur
To prick the sides of my intent, but only
Vaulting ambition, which o'erleaps itself
And falls on the other.
(Enter LADY MACBETH)
How now! what news?
Lady Macbeth. He has almost supp'd: why have you left the chamber?

(The characters freeze.)

Bill: This was it – the big one – the highly dramatic scene between two of the most famous murderers in literature, Macbeth and Lady Macbeth. I needed to pick two of my very best actors for this scene – two performers who were able to understand the complex characters involved and who would be able to create all of the tension and electricity that exists in one of the most highly charged interpersonal encounters ever written. And in order to capture and hold the attention of an audience that viewed bingo as the highlight of their existence, all of the motivations, intentions, timing, interplay, clarity of thought, vocalization and physical expression had to be just spot on.

Why have you left the chamber?

(They un-freeze.)

Macbeth. Hath he ask'd for me?
Lady Macbeth. Know you not he has?
Macbeth. We will proceed no further in this business:
He hath honour'd me of late; and I have bought
Golden opinions from all sorts of people,
Which would be worn now in their newest gloss,
Not cast aside so soon.
Lady Macbeth. Was the hope drunk
Wherein you dress'd yourself? hath it slept since?

And wakes it now, to look so green and pale
At what it did so freely? From this time
Such I account thy love. Art thou afeard
To be the same in thine own act and valour
As thou art in desire? Wouldst thou have that
Which thou esteem'st the ornament of life,
And live a coward in thine own esteem,
Letting 'I dare not' wait upon 'I would,'
Like the poor cat i' the adage?
Macbeth. Prithee, peace:
I dare do all that may become a man;
Who dares do more is none.
Lady Macbeth. What beast was't, then,
That made you break this enterprise to me?
When you durst do it, then you were a man;
And, to be more than what you were, you
      would
Be so much more the man. Nor time nor
      place
Did then adhere, and yet you would make
      both:
They have made themselves, and that their
      fitness now
Does unmake you. I have given suck, and
      know
How tender 'tis to love the babe that milks
      me:
I would, while it was smiling in my face,
Have pluck'd my nipple from his boneless
      gums,
And dash'd the brains out, had I so sworn as
      you
Have done to this.
Macbeth. If we should fail?
Lady Macbeth. We fail!
But screw your courage to the sticking-place,
And we'll not fail. When Duncan is asleep—
Whereto the rather shall his day's hard journey
Soundly invite him—his two chamberlains
Will I with wine and wassail so convince

That memory, the warder of the brain,
Shall be a fume, and the receipt of reason
A limbeck only: when in swinish sleep
Their drenched natures lie as in a death,
What cannot you and I perform upon
The unguarded Duncan? what not put upon
His spongy officers, who shall bear the guilt
Of our great quell?
Macbeth. Bring forth men-children only;
For thy undaunted mettle should compose
Nothing but males. Will it not be received,
When we have mark'd with blood those
      sleepy two
Of his own chamber and used their very
      daggers,
That they have done't?
Lady Macbeth. Who dares receive it other,
As we shall make our griefs and clamour roar
Upon his death?
Macbeth. I am settled, and bend up
Each corporal agent to this terrible feat.
Away, and mock the time with fairest show:
False face must hide what the false heart doth
      know.

Scene 5
(The tramps strike the scene to a bare stage as Bill concludes.)

Bill: The show had been a sensation, a roaring success. After that, the bookings started flooding in. I was looking forward to success and riches like I had never known before. But my cast had other ideas.

Tramp 1: No offence! It's been fun and we've learned loads about history and stuff. But it's not a proper job is it?

Bill: Isn't it?

Tramp 2: No – it's all right for a bit. But imagine having to do that night after night –

rehearsing play after play.

Tramp 3: We'd never cope – having to be co-ordinated and expressive all the time.

Tramp 4: Maintaining a responsive and flexible vocal instrument.

Tramp 2: Constantly performing the same lines, knowing what's going to happen, but keeping it fresh, believable, natural and spontaneous.

Tramp 3: Being truthful all the time, when really all you can think about is how you're going to pay the gas bill.

Tramp 1: No, not for us mate. Some people think it's easy. But not us.

Bill: But you just have to apply yourself to it, that's all – do some study – read some books – go to classes.

All good things must come to an end!

Tramp 1: See you, Bill. Thanks for the experience.

Tramps: *(variously)* Yeah, see you, bye, take care, so long.

(They exit as Bill goes centre stage, sits on his original crate and becomes Rosalind from As You Like It.*)*

Bill: I am not furnish'd like a beggar; therefore to beg will not become me. My way is to conjure you; and I'll begin with the women. I charge you, O women, for the love you bear to men, to like as much of this play as please you; and I charge you, O men, for the love you bear to women – as I perceive by your simp'ring none of you hates them – that between you and the women the play may please. If I were a woman, I would kiss as many of you as had beards that pleas'd me, complexions that lik'd me, and breaths that I defied not; and, I am sure, as many as have good beards, or good faces, or sweet breaths, will, for my kind offer, when I make curtsy, bid me farewell.

DOWN AND OUT – SOME NOTES ON THE SCENES

The Shakespearean extracts contained in this presentation present the actor with a variety and absorbing mix of challenges, which must be met with an equally varied armoury of techniques and skills.

Henry the Fifth

King Henry's rousing speech to his troops at the storming of the port of Harfleur in *Henry the Fifth*, Act III, scene i, is one of the most famous speeches in all of Shakespeare. There is a considerable technical challenge for the actor delivering this speech as it requires a series of builds and crescendos, arriving at an overall climax of dramatic fervour at the end. Not only does the actor require great power within the voice but an ability to control the breath and keep articulation sharp and responsive throughout. The speech should also be very physically engaged, encompassing large, sweeping and warlike gestures that must emanate from the actor's 'Centre'. Although this scene is often depicted with Henry on horseback, this is not so in this case, therefore care must be taken to keep 'weight down' and to remain physically relaxed as well as dynamic.

Henry the Fifth, Act II, scene iii, is dominated by an overwhelming sense of loss. However, this is not just the obvious loss of a much-loved companion, but also the loss of time: they mourn the passing not only of a person but of a period in their lives which that person represents and they stoically prepare for a new, much harsher time which they know is inevitable and which they face with a sense of determination. Although this wider loss is not directly mentioned, approaching the scene in the context of what has gone before, makes it an implicit part of the atmosphere of the scene. Therefore, it is essential for the actors involved to possess a deep knowledge and understanding of the play and of its themes.

The focal point of this scene is the wonderful speech of the Hostess (formerly known as

Actors discuss with the director in rehearsals.

Mistress Quickly and now married to Pistol). The actor playing this part must capture not only the great poetic sadness of the scene but also the practical, down-to-earth nature of the woman speaking it. It should be approached at an overall slow and lazy speed but also with regard to the fluctuation of pace and rhythmical ebb and flow between narration and speech quotation. It is also very important that the actor does not shy away from the comic implications in the very basic and direct description of her feeling slowly up Falstaff's prostrate body – discovering in a superbly matter-of-fact way that indeed 'all' was cold and lifeless. The key here is not to play the 'comedy' at all but to persist in the simplicity and truthfulness of the rendition at all times.

The men in the scene enhance the atmosphere with their beautifully delineated characters. Pistol, the head of the household, is ever practical – anxious to ensure that his wife is steadfast in her defence not only of the house but also of her honour while he is away at war.

The Boy should speak with an innocent charm, and Bardolph and Nym with straightforward but thoughtful directness. Nym, especially, should have a particular simplicity about his nature – not a man to become involved with the intimacy of kissing or outward shows of emotion, but equally moved by the situation in his own way.

The overall key to playing the scene is for each actor to listen and quietly react to each others words in the eulogy – allowing slow nods and smiles of recognition to pervade the quiet and poignant atmosphere.

As You Like It
As You Like It, Act III, scene iii, must surely contain some of Shakespeare's most incredibly colourful characters. Touchstone is a masterpiece of character writing and the actor portraying him must study hard to do justice to it. There is a wonderfully dry and practical element to his humour that must be encapsulated in a truly engagingly eccentric personality. One of the most important elements in his dialogue is the continual and relentless wordplay and punning and careful attention must be paid to working these through and understanding exactly what is being said and why. For example, he talks much of 'horns' and it must be understood that this is a standard reference to cuckolding and adultery. There is also a constant use of metaphor and simile that must be elucidated and his extraordinary but, somehow, logical outlook must be clarified: for instance, he would rather be married by a 'dodgy' priest so that although 'respectable' in marriage he will have more reason and excuse to extricate himself from it at a later date.

Audrey is deliciously funny and a rewarding part to play – a real country wench full of basic 'foulness', but also providing a 'straight-man like' foil to Touchstone's wit and humour. She 'feeds' him many of his funniest lines and jokes, and inadvertently provides him with a challenge to his intellectual reasoning. There is a lovely honest and self-deprecating aspect to Audrey's character in the way she speaks lines such as 'well, I am not fair, and therefore I pray the gods make me honest', and any actor should have tremendous fun in playing her.

Jaques is a fascinating character. He is removed from society both literally and metaphorically and from his safe and uninvolved vantage point he provides a wonderfully dry, witty and piercingly accurate commentary on

Jaques – life's observer.

the other participants in the story. The key to playing him in this scene is to focus upon his genuine fascination with the character and logic of Touchstone. He feels, perhaps, that he has, at last, met a fellow man with the intellectual ability to control life rather than be swamped by it. He is amused and intrigued by this and takes great pleasure in investigating and analysing the comic situation before him.

Although Sir Oliver Martext is a minor character in the overall scheme of the play, he is a gift of a cameo for any actor. As with many such characters, there is a variety of choice in the way he may be played – pompous, earnest, vague, drunk, or a combination of these and others. It is these beautifully-observed smaller parts that add so much depth and colour to

Shakespeare's plays, and the importance of playing them should never be underestimated.

Macbeth

There can be no doubt that high on the ambition list of all actors must be the desire to play Macbeth or Lady Macbeth. These are two of the most complex and fascinating roles that Shakespeare has to offer and in *Macbeth*, Act I, scene vii, we meet them at their most dramatically intriguing. There is a wonderful interplay to be had here between these two protagonists and this scene, and the play from which it comes, highlights, among other things, the importance of good casting. There is a tremendous chemistry between Macbeth and Lady Macbeth and the tension between them in this

153

scene demonstrates a struggle of power, sex, greed and determination. It is important that the actors playing these parts can find this chemistry between them and then develop the depth of passionate feeling that underpins the dialogue. It may well be that the use of improvisation, away from the text initially, will be of particular use here – not only in terms of the scene itself, but also in order to develop the relationship generally.

EXERCISE – BUILDING A RELATIONSHIP

Although this exercise principally involves the characters of Macbeth and Lady Macbeth, it is suitable to use with some, if not most, other pairings of characters and can be transposed accordingly. It is ideal for breaking down inhibitions between actors who may not know each other at the beginning of rehearsals and leading them towards the ultimate goal of creating a believable, truthful and dynamic relationship.

Part 1

Find a partner with whom to work. Find also a reasonably sized space in which to work.

Using chairs or other largish objects, create something of a maze by scattering them around the space. There should be enough room to move between them but the route from one end to the other should require turns and changes of direction.

One partner should be blindfolded. The other partner should now lead them through the maze, using only touch and without recourse to speech. In order to build trust, this must be done firmly and clearly, and it is important that the leading is not only achieved by holding hands and pulling but also by phys-

---

Handy Hint 26

Using Sound

A Shakespearean production may be greatly enhanced by using sound at various appropriate points in the action. This may be recorded sound, and it is possible to be extremely innovative in this area.

However, you will find that live sound is always very effective too. In this way, sound may become 'representative' in the same way that props and costume can be. For instance, having the cast make some kind of loud percussive noise (perhaps simply using dustbin lids or pots and pans) can very effectively create the atmosphere of war. This kind of device would be particularly effective for a production such as *Down and Out with Bill Shakespeare*.

Live music can also greatly enhance a production. It may be possible actually to have actors playing instruments at appropriate times in the play and this can really add to the experience as a whole.

---

ically turning the body and guiding by the shoulders when appropriate. The blindfold participant should feel totally secure, and this will require their guide to be very precise and reassuring with their physical guidance – directions must be confidently but gently executed.

Once the route through has been completed, without any bumps, you should change roles with your partner and repeat.

Now repeat this first part of the exercise but, this time, instead of using touch, voice only commands must be used. The blindfolded actor will now feel far more vulnerable than before and so the instructions must be even more precise and confident. Instructions should

The 'Trust Maze'.

be clear and simple and the recipient should obey each one slowly so as to give their guide ample time to ask them to stop and be still if they are about to bump an obstacle. When still, the recipient should wait patiently until the guide has reassessed the next move and speaks the next command. It must be a rule that only the guide may speak so, if an instruction is unclear, their partner must not move until the command has been rephrased intelligibly.

Once again, change roles and repeat.

This part of the exercise is also very useful as an ice-breaker when a cast or group starts to work together for the first time as it is very successful in getting people relating to each other and abandoning inhibitions and shyness. However, the atmosphere must remain calm and giggling and chat should be kept to a minimum so that those undertaking the exercise can concentrate and feel safe.

Part 2

Both actors should now devise a physical activity to undertake. This can be dusting the room, moving chairs from one side to the other or anything else that requires them to move and continue in the pursuit of a simple task.

As this is being done, a series of discussions should be initiated using each of the subjects from the following list in turn, with each participant taking a distinct and opposing view to the other. Each individual discussion should continue until it is deemed that one or other of the participants has won the argument before moving on to the next item on the list. (It will be helpful for you to enlist the services of a third actor to act as umpire if possible.) As you will see, each discussion grows not only in its emotional intensity from the last but also in its personal relevance. Do not feel it necessary at the start to relate to each other as sexual partners in particular, just let the relationship grow as each discussion has its effect. The list itself will sculpture the relationship correctly. The movement and task will help to allow the argument to build naturally and defuse some of the tension early on but, as the discussion becomes more vibrant and reaches its climax, this can be abandoned in favour of direct physical confrontation.

* What colour should the room be painted?
* What should be cooked for supper?
* Should private education be abolished?
* Is capitalism wrong?
* Should capital punishment be restored?
* Is infidelity forgivable?
* Which of us should go out to work?
* Should the female's mother be put into a home?
* Do you still love each other?
* Should the male murder his boss in order to take his job?

As you will see the final discussion leads the improvisation right back to the scene and the play, ready for the next part of the exercise.

Part 3

You should now refer to the actual text of *Macbeth*, Act I, scene vii. Each should have a copy of the dialogue for reference, but the words should be learned for the exercise if at all possible – if time will not allow this for the first attempt, then you could return to the exercise on another occasion when there has been time for study. Make sure, as usual, that you understand every-

Highlight the conflict.

thing that you are actually saying in the scene.

Both sit either side of a small table. Place your elbows upon the table and link hands.

Now play the scene while arm wrestling. However, do not only allow strength of arm to dictate progress of the fight but, rather, use the ebb and flow of the verbal sparring to mirror itself physically in the similar thrust and parry of the arm movements. If you feel that Macbeth is convincing in his speeches then his wife's hand may be pushed towards the table surface. However, as she counters his objections so forcefully, the reverse should happen, leading at last to a victory.

CONCLUSION

Have fun!

Having completed reading this book and, hopefully, having worked hard upon the exercises that it contains, you should consider yourself not at an 'end' but at a 'beginning'. You should now continue your studies, developing, and adding to your programme of exercises from other sources and generally stretching and extending your skills as you move forwards.

Most importantly, you should, if you have not done so already, get out there and start to perform Shakespeare in whatever capacity is appropriate to your situation. Whether you be an amateur, professional or student, the very least you should do now is gather together a group of colleagues, find a venue (the local hall will do), pick a play (perhaps start with one of the comedies) rehearse and then perform it.

The main thing to remember is to be inventive and have fun with the text. Agree upon an appropriate and innovative interpretation for your chosen play; be resourceful and imaginative in your provision of costume, props and set; use the performance space effectively (don't just use the stage but sometimes the audience area as well); and then find out what you think the text means and play it for all your worth.

Just enjoy – if you do, so will the audience!

FURTHER READING

Barton, John, *Playing Shakespeare* (Methuen Drama, July 1984)

Bicât, Tina, *Period Costume for the Stage* (The Crowood Press, 2001)

Doyle, John, and Ray Lischner, *Shakespeare for Dummies* (John Wiley & Sons, April 1999)

Hall, Peter, *Shakespeare's Advice to the Players* (Oberon Books, April 2004)

Hester, John, *Stage Acting Techniques* (The Crowood Press, 2004)

Hester, John, *Understanding and Researching Scripts* (The Crowood Press, 2006)

Lloyd Evans, Gareth and Barbara, *Companion to Shakespeare* (J.M. Dent & Sons Ltd, 1978)

Perry, John, *The Rehearsal Handbook* (The Crowood Press, 2001)

Rodenburg, Patsy, *Speaking Shakespeare* (Methuen Drama, April 2005)

Wells, Stanley, *A Dictionary of Shakespeare* (Oxford University Press, 1998)

INDEX